# CONTENTS

# HUMAN TRAFFICKING: MAIL ORDER BRIDE ABUSES

---

**TUESDAY, JULY 13, 2004**

U.S. SENATE,
SUBCOMMITTEE ON EAST ASIAN
AND PACIFIC AFFAIRS,
COMMITTEE ON FOREIGN RELATIONS,
*Washington, DC.*

The subcommittee met at 3:02 p.m., in room SD–419, Dirksen Senate Office Building, Hon. Sam Brownback (chairman of the subcommittee), presiding.

Present: Senator Brownback.

OPENING STATEMENT OF SENATOR SAM BROWNBACK

Senator BROWNBACK. I call the subcommittee hearing to order.

Thank you very much for joining us today. We have got three panels and a short period of time to do this in. I have an hour that we can conduct this hearing. So we will need to move through very vigorously.

Today we will be hearing from three panels on the issues surrounding international marriage brokers, so-called mail order brides, and the links that can be made to human trafficking. I am please to welcome my colleague and friend, who will soon appear, Senator Maria Cantwell from the great State of Washington, to be our first panel. Senator Cantwell has seen abuses against mail order brides occur in her own State and has authored the International Marriage Brokers Regulation Act. Her passion for protecting women trapped in such abusive and dangerous relationships is to be commended.

On our second panel, we have with us former Washington State Congressman, John Miller, who is Director of the Office to Monitor and Combat Trafficking in Persons from the State Department. He has done exemplary work on the issue of trafficking and has gained international respect and recognition for that.

On our third panel, we are pleased to have several experts on the issue of human trafficking who will present their views.

The problem of human trafficking has garnered significant support and attention over the past few years. Just last September before the United Nations, President Bush's words represented a truly historic moment in the war to free the millions of innocent human beings who suffer as slaves in the sex industry or in other forms of forced labor. Both the Trafficking Victims Protection Act of 2000 and the Trafficking Victims Reauthorization Act of 2003 have indicated major steps by the U.S. Congress to eradicate this form of slavery.

Today's hearing will focus specifically on the topic of international marriage brokers and international matchmaking organizations, IMO's, who facilitate the exchange between mail sponsors and female mail order brides. Senator Cantwell knows all too well the story of Anastasia King, a mail order bride who was abused and eventually murdered by her sponsor husband. Several reports and news articles have indicated in recent years the disturbing trend of mail order brides who suffer from domestic abuse. In addition to the reports of domestic abuse, several of our witnesses here today will speak to the connection between human trafficking, organized crime, and these matchmaking industries.

It is my hope that this hearing will serve to educate us in the Senate, bring awareness and attention to the issue, and propel it forward in considering how best to protect the many victims of abuse and trafficking that have arrived through seemingly legitimate matchmaking organizations.

I want to describe just one story of one victim. I will not put forth her name to protect her identity. I will submit her full written statement for the record.

[The statement referred to follows:]

A VICTIM'S STORY

I swear this statement is true.

I was born in the capital city of Ethiopia. I am 29 years old. I have two younger brothers. My mom is a strong and courageous woman who supports her family and sacrifices her life for her children. My father was passed away for long time ago. My mom is an accountant and my father was a teacher. I have a very good family and I was so happy.

I was grown up in a big city in Addis Ababa. 2.5 million people are living in Addis Ababa. I went different schools for elementary and secondary class.

I joined a college and working in part time. My mom help me half of my tuition and I paid half of it. My mom did this for me and for my younger brother to help us to be educated.

One after noon when I went to the library to study and also I was missed one class so I just try to find if some one had a class note. I want to look at it before I will go to class. That is the beginning of my new story. I was asking a girl. She was at in the library at that time to borrow her class note and look at it. When I got her exercise book. I found a lot of men picture and it describes their age, weight, height, hobby, profession and so on. They want to meet some one for relationship. I never heard and saw it before. I knew something about pen pal. Pen pal you can buy from different organization or you can find without cost and it is different from this dating service. She explained it to me. She said it is the same like pen pal you can write them its good for your English and it is fun. I am not the only one that day to saw those picture. This was around exam time I remembered. She photocopied and gave it to me. We just pick what ever we want even most of us pick the same person. It was not a big deal in a foreign country to whom one writes letters but whom one has never met in person. I never heard in my whole life some one married or get a boy friend from dating service.

After the exam it was winter. In Ethiopia June, July, and August are winter and the school all over the country will closed. I get the address on May but I didn't write. I even did not think about it. When I was to sell my old book. I found it again. I decided to write and I did. He described him self and his profession is a consultant. I started writing a letter by describing my self and included my picture that was it from the beginning.

After three weeks I received two letters from him including his picture. He described him self-different in his first letter for me. He said he is a doctor. He does not want to say it the truth about his profession on those dating services. I went to show to my friends. Because his reaction is so fast. I always received a letter from him including his picture and business card every time. He also asked me to call

S. HRG. 108–695

# HUMAN TRAFFICKING: MAIL ORDER BRIDE ABUSES

## HEARING

BEFORE THE

SUBCOMMITTEE ON EAST ASIAN AND PACIFIC AFFAIRS

OF THE

COMMITTEE ON FOREIGN RELATIONS
UNITED STATES SENATE

ONE HUNDRED EIGHTH CONGRESS

SECOND SESSION

JULY 13, 2004

Printed for the use of the Committee on Foreign Relations

Available via the World Wide Web: http://www.access.gpo.gov/congress/senate

U.S. GOVERNMENT PRINTING OFFICE

96–804 PDF WASHINGTON : 2004

For sale by the Superintendent of Documents, U.S. Government Printing Office
Internet: bookstore.gpo.gov Phone: toll free (866) 512–1800; DC area (202) 512–1800
Fax: (202) 512–2250 Mail: Stop SSOP, Washington, DC 20402–0001

## COMMITTEE ON FOREIGN RELATIONS

RICHARD G. LUGAR, Indiana, *Chairman*

CHUCK HAGEL, Nebraska
LINCOLN CHAFEE, Rhode Island
GEORGE ALLEN, Virginia
SAM BROWNBACK, Kansas
MICHAEL B. ENZI, Wyoming
GEORGE V. VOINOVICH, Ohio
LAMAR ALEXANDER, Tennessee
NORM COLEMAN, Minnesota
JOHN E. SUNUNU, New Hampshire

JOSEPH R. BIDEN, JR., Delaware
PAUL S. SARBANES, Maryland
CHRISTOPHER J. DODD, Connecticut
JOHN F. KERRY, Massachusetts
RUSSELL D. FEINGOLD, Wisconsin
BARBARA BOXER, California
BILL NELSON, Florida
JOHN D. ROCKEFELLER IV, West Virginia
JON S. CORZINE, New Jersey

KENNETH A. MYERS, JR., *Staff Director*
ANTONY J. BLINKEN, *Democratic Staff Director*

---

## SUBCOMMITTEE ON EAST ASIAN AND PACIFIC AFFAIRS

SAM BROWNBACK, Kansas, *Chairman*

LAMAR ALEXANDER, Tennessee
CHUCK HAGEL, Nebraska
GEORGE ALLEN, Virginia
GEORGE V. VOINOVICH, Ohio

JOHN F. KERRY, Massachusetts
JOHN D. ROCKEFELLER IV, West Virginia
RUSSELL D. FEINGOLD, Wisconsin
JON S. CORZINE, New Jersey

him. It so expensive for me to call him. I said I couldn't call you. He asked my phone number. I wrote and sent it to him. Then he started calling me every other day, night, day midnight it was so interesting. He told me he love. For me personally it was so funny and I do not know what is going on. When he said I love you, I did too. I was sure I would never see him in person. He is from far so I do not care to say I love you. It was fun to my younger brother to answer his phone too just to took in English.

He was serious and sends me every time money, clothes and different kinds of gifts. He also asked to marry him. I said yes. I was sure I would never see him. He will never come. When be sends a weeding dress I was so scared. It was impossible to me some one interested in me even he do not know me in person.

He came finally. He was handsome, seems a good Christian, carrying, generous and loving person. I was asked him why he was interested in me and why he didn't married in his country. He told me every one want him because he is a doctor and has a lot of money not for love. I thought he really want a good marriage. I felt I was blessed. I do not have any reason to stop marrying him it was so blessing to met some one perfect in my eyes for that time. I married him. Every one was so happy for me and it was just like a dream. We had a very good time. He told me he will going to apply a visa for me to come to united states. The Visa he wants to apply was a fiancé visa. He explained it takes only a few months. He said it is easy and it doesn't take long time. He said if he apply marriage visa it takes more than a year. I do not have any idea about visa. I was agreeing with him what ever he said. I knew he care for me and he is also smart and knew everything about his country.

American embassy sends me visa application. After a few months he left. I was scanning and email every document I got from American embassy because he asked me to do it. He filled all the application and sent it to me to return back to American embassy in Ethiopia. Finally I got a visa. I was planning to stay a little bit longer before I leave. I have to get done a lot of things. But he made me hurry. I came after I got a visa two weeks. I was happy and I can't wait to see him and to live with him.

Second part of my story was so scary. I never expect from him this king of reaction. I was stayed in his house for three days. He is so different. He started abused me physically and mentally. I was so confused. I didn't believe what was happened. I was so scared to death. He drugged me too sleep long hour. I knew my life is in danger and it will be over. I can read from his eyes. The way he looks at me was so different and he gave me wrong information about American people. He told me to stay in the bedroom. He told me in this country if some one killed some one and has a lot of money. He will never go to prison. He showed me a lot of scary movies. I was cried every day and waiting death. He told me if I went out side and the police found me. They will arrest me and put me in Jail. He told me before I came do not bring money and clothes. But I did and he was so mad and spent all my money. He also had my passport. I do not have any identification with me.

We stayed almost five places with in a month that was so scary too because it seems he try to hid him self. Even he told me I will arrested and go to prison if the police found me. I prefer to stay in jail rather than dying. At that moment we were stayed in motel. I went out to took to front desk to asked help and they called to the police. The police took me to the women shelter. After a few days he killed him self.

With in a month my life is up side down. I do not know what going to happen next and I do not want to go back home because I was experienced most of Ethiopian didn't respect a widower. I knew it because my mom is a widower too. I was just lost and sick. Here I am with out a closure what was happened and anger, depression, guilt. I do not have answer for this all my question and I will carry this all for the rest of my life.

Name withheld.

Senator BROWNBACK. This one particular bride, so to speak, a native of Ethiopia, was introduced to the concept of matchmaking organizations through an acquaintance at school. While in college, she decided to practice her English by sending an e-mail to her new pen pal. She immediately received pictures and letters of this man and soon thereafter he started calling her. Eventually she received money and clothes and then a marriage proposal. Throughout their Internet courtship, she never believed there was a future for her in the United States. However, 2 weeks after her visa was completed, she arrived in the United States and married the man she had corresponded with for several months.

Upon arrival in the United States, the victim's dreams of the fairy tale marriage to a caring and loving husband began to unravel when she was forced to stay in the house for the first 3 days. Then he began abusing her both physically and mentally. Her new husband, an anesthesiologist, drugged her, forcing her to stay in the bedroom. Her own words profoundly express the fear that she suffered. "He showed me a lot of scary movies. I cried every day and waiting for death. He told me if I went outside and the police found me, they will arrest me and put me in jail. He told me before I came, do not bring money and clothes, but I did and he was so mad and spent all my money. He also had my passport. I do not have any identification with me. We stayed in almost five places within a month that was so scary too because it seems he tried to hide himself."

Eventually this victim was able to escape and found a women's shelter. Her husband killed himself. She says of the experience, "Here I am without a closure what has happened and angry and depressed and guilty. I do not have answer for this all my question and I will carry this all for the rest of my life."

This victim was able to present ample evidence demonstrating that her husband brought her to the United States under fraudulent claims, and that he tortured her for several weeks indicating that he intended only to use her as a sex slave. She was granted a T-visa and was able to receive much needed medical and psychological care. And I am pleased to report that she lives, attends college, and works in her community today. The emotional and physical trauma that she endured will, indeed, affect the rest of her life, but I commend her strength and integrity for sharing her personal tragedy with us. There are many other victims who have been silenced by similar abuse.

I recognize the many legitimate matchmaking organizations and do not wish to undermine them, but I hope that many of the IMOs that make themselves available on our Internet today will also take an initiative to protect women from abuse and potential trafficking.

I want to thank you all for being here today. I want to particularly recognize and thank the Honorable Maria Cantwell, who put forward this legislation that hopefully we will be able to consider and pass by this committee and get it moving forward, and for her testimony here today. Senator Cantwell.

## STATEMENT OF HON. MARIA CANTWELL, U.S. SENATOR FROM WASHINGTON

Senator CANTWELL. Thank you, Mr. Chairman, and thank you for this opportunity to address the committee and I certainly appreciate your interest in this issue that is of growing epidemic proportions. I certainly look forward to working with you and the committee on Senate bill 1455 or various additions or versions of Senate bill 1455 that might be able to make its way through the U.S. Senate. So again, thank you for this opportunity.

I also want to thank you for working with me to help bring the nexus recognition between human trafficking and the problems of international marriage brokers, and I would like to say quickly that I had the pleasure last week of meeting with former Congressman John Miller, Director of the State Department Office to Monitor and Combat Trafficking in Persons. The Trafficking Victims Protection Reauthorization Act, passed by Congress and signed by the President last December, actually raises the specter of Congressman Miller's position to the rank of Ambassador-at-Large, calling for an appointment by the President with the advice and consent of the Senate. So I hope that Congressman Miller's presence here today will help expedite his speedy consideration by this committee and hope that the Senate gives his nomination a speedy approval.

Human trafficking is the politic way of describing of what is really modern-day slavery. Last month the U.S. State Department Office to Monitor and Combat Trafficking in Persons released a new report estimating that between 800,000 and 900,000 men, women, and children are trafficked across international borders every year. The report estimates that 18,000 to 20,000 people are trafficked into the United States each year.

When we talk about human trafficking and abuse, we need to be aware of the advent of for-profit international marriage brokers, companies that operate solely to connect men and women of different nations with the intent of getting married.

The use of these marriage broker services has exploded in recent years with the growth of the Internet. Web sites such as www.goodwife.com, www.womenrussia.com, and www.filipinaladies.com tout young women looking for love and marriage. In 1999 the Immigration and Naturalization Service commissioned a study that found that more than 200 international marriage broker operations were operating around the globe, arranging between 4,000 and 6,000 marriages between American men and foreign women every year. Today experts put the number of international marriage brokers at nearly 500 worldwide. And based on 1999 statistics, there are between 20,000 and 30,000 women who have entered the United States using an international marriage broker in the last 5 years.

Unfortunately, women meeting their husbands through brokers frequently have little opportunity to get to know their prospective spouse or assess the potential for violence. They also have little knowledge of their rights as victims of domestic violence in our country even if they are not yet citizens or permanent residents. And tragically it is becoming apparent that there is a growing epidemic of domestic violence and abuse among couples who met via international marriage brokers. Immigrant groups and women advocacy groups across the country report seeing an increase in the number of these wives seeking to escape physical abuse from husbands that they met through international marriage brokers. And in several cases, the abuse has progressed to murder.

In my home State of Washington, we know of at least two cases of women who met their husbands through Internet-based international marriage brokers. The first one, Susanna Blackwell, met her husband, Timothy Blackwell, through an international marriage broker, and in 1994, left her native Philippines to move to Washington to marry him. During their short marriage, Mr. Blackwell physically abused his wife regularly. Within a few months, Susanna decided to leave her husband and started divorce proceedings. The Blackwells had been separated for more than a year, and on the last day of the divorce proceeding, Mr. Blackwell shot and killed Susanna and two of her friends who were waiting outside the Seattle courtroom.

In 1999, an 18-year-old Anastasia Solovyova married Indle King, a man she met through an international marriage broker. Entries from Anastasia's diary detail the abuse she suffered at the hands of her husband and how she feared him. According to Anastasia's diary, Mr. King threatened Anastasia with death if she were to leave him, and unfortunately in December of 2000, that threat came through when Indle King killed Anastasia.

At trial, it was discovered that Mr. King had previously married another woman that he had met through an international marriage broker organization. His first wife instituted a domestic violence protection order against Mr. King prior to divorcing him in 1997, some information that was not made available to Anastasia King when she entered the United States.

Sadly there are similar examples of violence across the country of women who have met their American spouses through Internet-based marriage brokers only to be seriously injured or killed by an American spouse with a preexisting history of violence against women.

In response to those cases, I have introduced the International Marriage Broker Regulation Act, S. 1455. The legislation is modeled on groundbreaking legislation passed in the State of Washington related to trafficking of persons and called the mail order bride legislation.

The primary goal of the legislation is to better inform women entering this country as to the prospects of their spouse and past activity and domestic violence history prior to them coming to the United States and marrying the individuals.

The bill would first halt the current practice of allowing Americans to simultaneously seek visas for multiple fiancées by requiring that only one fiancée visa may be sought per applicant each year. What we are finding in many of these cases is that men put in for many, many different women at the same time coming to the United States.

Currently multiple requests for fiancée visas can be simultaneously filed with the Bureau of Citizenship and Immigration, and the American requesting the visa will simply choose to marry the first woman who is approved.

Second, the international marriage broker legislation would require that brokers would be required to ask American clients to provide information on previous arrests, convictions, or court order restrictions relating to crimes of violence, along with previous marital history. This information would also be made available to the foreign national.

Finally, the legislation would require a U.S. citizen seeking a foreign fiancée visa to undergo a criminal background check, a check that is already performed for the fiancée entering the United

States. Information on convictions and civil orders would be relayed to the visa applicant by the consular official, along with information of their legal rights should they find themselves in an abusive relationship.

Today an American seeking to marry someone through an international marriage broker holds all the cards. The American client has the benefit of a complete background check on his future wife, which is a requirement of the immigration process. In addition, the brokers provide clients extensive information about the women they offer, everything from favorite hobbies to movies and other past activities.

Conversely, the foreign fiancée only gets whatever information her future spouse wants to share. These women have no way of confirming what they are told about the previous marriages or relationships or the client's criminal history.

Most of the foreign brides advertised by the international brokers come from countries where women are oppressed, have few educational and professional opportunities, and in some cases are countries where domestic violence against women is condoned, if not encouraged. Because of the cultural differences, researchers say there is an inherent imbalance of power in these relationships between American men and foreign women.

Senate bill 1455 would give foreign fiancées critical information they need to make informed decisions about the person whom they plan to marry. It puts these foreign brides on more equal footing with their American grooms.

Mr. Chairman, I thank you for the opportunity to address this issue before the committee, and I look forward to working with you on ways that we might foster the freedom and free will of individuals throughout the world who are brought here to the United States.

[The prepared statement of Senator Cantwell follows:]

PREPARED STATEMENT OF SENATOR MARIA CANTWELL

Mr. Chairman, thank you for inviting me to testify before the committee today. I also want to thank you for working with me to bring recognition to the nexus between human trafficking and problems with international marriage brokers.

I would like to say, quickly, that I had the pleasure of meeting with John Miller, Director of the State Department's Office to Monitor and Combat Trafficking in Persons, just last week. The Trafficking Victims Protection Reauthorization Act, passed by Congress and signed by the President last December 19, actually raises the specter of Mr. Miller's position to the rank of Ambassador-at-Large, calling for an appointment by the President with the advice and consent of the Senate. Having received the appointment, I would also like to say that I hope for a speedy consent to John's nomination.

Human trafficking is the politic way of describing modern-day slavery. Last month the U.S. State Department's Office to Monitor and Combat Trafficking in Persons released a new report estimating that between 800,000 and 900,000 men, women, and children are trafficked across international borders every year. The report estimates that 18,000 and 20,000 people are trafficked into the United States each year.

When we talk about human trafficking and abuse, we need to also be aware of the advent of for-profit international marriage brokers [IMBs]—companies that operate solely to connect men and women of different nations with the intent of getting married.

The use of these marriage broker services has exploded in recent years with the growth of the Internet. Web sites such as *www.goodwife.com; www.womenrussia.com* and *www.filipinaladies.com* tout young women looking for love and marriage. In 1999 the Immigration and Naturalization Service commissioned a study that found more than 200 IMBs operating around the globe, arranging between 4,000 and 6,000 marriages between American men and foreign women every year. Today, experts put the number of international marriage brokers at nearly 500 worldwide. And based on the 1999 statistics, there are between 20,000 and 30,000 women who have entered the U.S. using an international marriage broker in the past five years. While there are a few brokers aimed at American female clients who are seeking male spouses from other countries, the overwhelming majority of people who seek IMB services are men.

Unfortunately, women meeting their husbands through brokers frequently have little opportunity to get to know their prospective spouses or assess their potential for violence. They also have little knowledge of their rights as victims of domestic violence in our country, even if they are not yet citizens or permanent residents. And tragically, it is becoming apparent that there is a growing epidemic of domestic abuse among couples who meet via international marriage brokers. Immigrant and women's advocacy groups across the country report seeing an increase in the number of these wives seeking to escape a physically abusive husband they met through an IMB. And in several cases, the abuse has progressed to murder.

In my home state of Washington, we know of at least three cases of serious domestic violence including two murders of women who met their husbands through Internet-based international marriage brokers.

Susanna Blackwell met her husband, Timothy Blackwell, through an international marriage broker and, in 1994, left her native Philippines to move to Washington to marry him. During their short marriage, Mr. Blackwell physically abused his wife regularly. Within a few months, Susanna decided to leave her husband and started divorce proceedings. The Blackwells had been separated for more than a year when Mr. Blackwell learned Susanna was eight-months pregnant with another man's child. On the last day of the divorce proceedings, Mr. Blackwell shot and killed Susanna, her unborn child, and two friends who were waiting outside of the Seattle courtroom.

In 1999, 18-year-old Anastasia Solovyova married Indle King, a man she met through an international marriage broker. Entries from Anastasia's diary detail the abuse she suffered at the hands of her husband and the fear she had for him. According to Anastasia's diary, Mr. King threatened Anastasia with death if she were to leave him; and, in December 2000, this threat came true.

At trial, it was discovered that Mr. King had been previously married to another woman he met through an Internet-based IMB, as well, a woman who instituted a domestic violence protection order against Mr. King prior to divorcing him in 1997. It was also discovered that he was seeking his third wife through another international marriage broker when he developed the plot to kill Anastasia.

Sadly, there are similar examples across the country of women who have met their American spouses through an Internet-based marriage broker only to be seriously injured or killed by an American spouse with a pre-existing history of violence against women.

In response to these cases, I introduced the International Marriage Broker Regulation Act (S. 1455). This legislation is modeled on a series of groundbreaking Washington State laws related to trafficking of persons and "mail order brides."

The primary goal of my legislation is to better inform women entering this country as a prospective spouse about the past history of the man she may be marrying and to better inform them of their rights as residents of the United States if they become victims of domestic violence.

The bill would, first, halt the current practice of allowing Americans to simultaneously seek visas for multiple fiancées by requiring that only one fiancée visa may be sought per applicant each year. Currently, multiple requests for fiancée visas can be simultaneously filed with the Bureau of Citizenship and Immigration, and the American requesting the visa will simply choose to marry the first woman who is approved.

Second, my bill would require that, before an international marriage broker may release the contact information of a foreign national client, the broker must first obtain her consent to the release of that information and provide her with information, in her own language, on the rights of victims of domestic violence in this country.

Third, the international marriage broker would be required to ask American clients to provide information on any previous arrest, conviction or court-ordered restriction relating to crimes of violence along with their previous marital history. This information would also be made available to the foreign national.

Finally, it would require a U.S. citizen seeking a foreign fiancée visa to undergo a criminal background check, a check that is already performed for the fiancées entering the country themselves. Information on convictions and civil orders would be relayed to the visa applicant by the consular official along with information on their legal rights should they find themselves in an abusive relationship.

Today, an American seeking to marry someone through an international marriage broker holds all of the cards. The American client has the benefit of a complete background check on his future wife, which is a requirement of the immigration process. In addition, the brokers provide clients extensive information about the women they offer, everything from their favorite movies and hobbies to whether they are sexually promiscuous.

Conversely, the foreign fiancée only gets whatever information her future spouse wants to share. These women have no way of confirming what they are told about previous marriages or relationships—or the American client's criminal history.

Most of the foreign brides advertised by the international marriage brokers come from countries where women are oppressed, have few educational or professional opportunities, and where violence against women is condoned, if not encouraged. Because of the cultural differences, researchers say there is an inherent imbalance of power in these relationships between American men and foreign women.

Because these women often immigrate alone, they have no family or other support network and rely on their husbands for everything. Such dependency can make it difficult for a wife to report abuse without worrying that doing so is a surefire ticket to deportation. Researchers agree that isolation and dependency put these women at greater risk of domestic abuse.

Documenting the extent of this problem has been quite difficult. Marriages arranged by brokers are not tracked separately from other immigrant marriages. However, experts agree that abuse is more likely in such arranged marriages and that abuse in these relationships is likely underreported since the women are likely to be more afraid of deportation than the abuse they suffer at home.

My legislation would give foreign fiancées critical information they need to make an informed decision about the person whom they plan to marry. It puts these foreign brides on more equal footing with their American grooms.

Thank you, again, for this opportunity to come before you and address the unique intersection of trafficking of persons and the use of international marriage brokers. I look forward to working with all of you so that we might foster the freedom and free will of individuals throughout the world and here at home in the United States.

Senator BROWNBACK. Thank you, Senator Cantwell, and thank you for your work on this.

One question just pops out immediately. Why would a foreign bride do this? Why would she come with that lack of information? As you have visited with some of the women who have been caught in this type of situation, why would they even subject themselves to these possibilities?

Senator CANTWELL. These women oftentimes come from very poor economic circumstances. The family of Anastasia King shared with me the stories of their daughter's hopes and dreams of coming to America. Often the daughter represents a link to a new opportunity in America that perhaps once this union is brought together, that maybe there are other opportunities for other family members. So while I think the Anastasia King family was very anxious about her situation of going abroad and marrying, they thought that it was the best way for her to have economic opportunity in the future and perhaps thought that there might be a day and time in which they might join her in America.

Senator BROWNBACK. And that seems to be the pretty consistent theme that you see coming forward of why people would be willing to subject themselves with a lack of data or information that they might have about the husband they would be marrying in the United States?

Senator CANTWELL. I do not know of any wealthy, well-educated, well-to-do women who have applied for these brokered licenses.

Senator BROWNBACK. Thank you very much, Senator Cantwell, for your presentation, for your push on this topic. I think it is incredibly important and I appreciate your diligence in moving it forward.

Senator CANTWELL. Thank you, Mr. Chairman. I look forward to working with you on the issue.

Senator BROWNBACK. Same here.

Next, on our second panel, we will hear from the Honorable John Miller. He is the Director of the Trafficking in Persons Office at the Department of State. Director and hopefully soon-to-be Ambassador Miller, I look forward to your presentation.

**STATEMENT OF HON. JOHN R. MILLER, DIRECTOR, OFFICE TO MONITOR AND COMBAT TRAFFICKING IN PERSONS, U.S. DEPARTMENT OF STATE**

Mr. MILLER. Thank you, Senator. First, I want to salute both you and Senator Cantwell. I want to salute you for your work over the years on this premier 21st century human rights issue, slavery, and all that you have done. I want to salute Senator Cantwell, a Senator from my home State, for taking the lead with this Senate bill 1455 to address an important component of the slavery issue. I think you are both to be commended.

Fortunately, we have on the next panel some distinguished NGO witnesses who have worked with this issue and will have some specific illustrations of what is involved.

I want to focus, if I can, on the worldwide perspective here. When you look at the slavery issue, we now have reason to believe that 80 percent of the millions that are in slavery, internal or external traffic victims, 80 percent are women and 50 percent are children. The two biggest categories are sex slavery and probably domestic servitude. I think these are two of the categories of slavery that you frequently have that victims that you and Senator Cantwell have described end up in.

What do we know about trafficked victims in general? Well, there are two or three characteristics. There is the vulnerability of the victims. Senator Cantwell alluded to that. There is the deception, the key tool of the traffickers, and often there is government complicity and corruption. Well, if you look at marriage brokering, you have these features, particularly the first two features, the vulnerability of the women and the deception involved. These are features that we have to deal with.

What we are talking about here, of course, are individuals. Research is hard to come by in terms of generalizations or numbers on this issue, but we know from rural villages in Asia to slums in major South American cities, women are deceived into leaving their homes and traveling across international borders in the hopes of marrying men who can provide them better lives.

Sometimes the traffickers recruit the victims through direct offers on the spot. I am going to give an example of that. Sometimes there is negotiating through a member of the family, a broker. Sometimes it is through newspaper or mail or the Internet. Invariably there is a cash payment involved.

Let me just give one example because this is somebody I met in Cambodia. I visited a faith-based shelter, the White Lotus, in Phnom Penh, and while there, I met a woman who appeared to me to be very elderly. I was told that she was dying of sexually transmitted diseases. She did not have long to live, and I asked her to tell me her story.

Pou—that was her name—said that at the age of 17, a man had come to her rural village in Cambodia and arranged through her sister to marry her. The day after the marriage, the man, the "husband," took Pou to another village, a fishing village, where he said he was going to go to work. He took her to a hotel or what she thought was a hotel. She woke up the next morning. Her husband was gone. The hotel turned out to be a brothel. She had been sold, sold into captivity. After threats and beatings, she was told she had to pay off this huge debt, the purchase price, before she had any hope of freedom. She spent years "servicing" men.

She finally was released not because she had paid off the debt. She was released because she had been ravaged by disease and the brothel considered her disposable. They just threw her out on the street basically. She wandered to Phnom Penh where she found this shelter.

At the end of the interview, I looked at this elderly woman and I said, how old are you? And she said to me, 24. That is what had happened in the course of 7 years.

In some villages in South Asia, they are now taking Polaroid photographs of men who come to communities and take a bride and posting the photographs in nearby villages because they are so concerned of this multiple operation. This man who took Pou I am sure had done that scores of times and was going to do it scores of times again. It gets to the dialog Senator Cantwell and you had about seeking multiple fiancées.

Well, those photos—that is a good technique where there is a direct operation. But of course, we are dealing here with methods that are far from direct. You are dealing, when you are talking about the United States and women coming from abroad, with the mail, you are dealing with newspaper advertisements, you are dealing primarily with the Internet. You are dealing with marriage brokers, legal brokers, who for a fee introduce prospective brides to wealthier foreign men and, unfortunately in a significant number of cases, facilitate trafficking in persons.

We know, as I say, this is going on all over the world. Just to give another example, we receive reports there is extensive trafficking of women from Vietnam to Taiwan. They are married to Taiwanese men, and then when they are transported to Taiwan, they end up in the brothels. I mentioned examples from Asia, Cambodia, Taiwan, Vietnam, but it is a worldwide phenomenon. Just as trafficking not only extends to other countries in the world and extends to the United States, we can say that this form of trafficking, as you have heard from the examples from the State of Washington given by Senator Cantwell, extends to this country.

So I applaud your efforts, Mr. Chairman, and Senator Cantwell's efforts to tighten oversight of marriage brokers operating in the United States in order to prevent the abuse of vulnerable women and children. Thank you.

[The prepared statement of Mr. Miller follows:]

PREPARED STATEMENT OF HON. JOHN R. MILLER

EXPLORING POTENTIAL LINKS BETWEEN HUMAN TRAFFICKING AND INTERNATIONAL MARRIAGE BROKERING

Thank you, Mr. Chairman. It is an honor to appear before you. You have devoted great energy to making America a leader in the global effort to eradicate trafficking in persons, and you have made a tremendous difference in the lives of many people around the world. I salute you for your humanitarian work.

I also salute Senator Cantwell for her humanitarian concern and for introducing the International Marriage Broker Regulation Act.

Today, as we approach the topic of international marriage brokering and its potential links to human trafficking, it is important for us to remember the humanity of the trafficking issue—not just the legalities—because it is, after all, real people we seek to protect.

I have met men, women, and children around the world who have been recruited, deceived, forced, and coerced into unimaginable situations where they are deprived of their freedom, stripped of their dignity, and abused into hopelessness. I have seen and heard of people who have been bought and sold into domestic servitude, commercial sexual exploitation, child soldiering, forced labor, and camel jockeying. These modern-day forms of slavery are brutal not just to the minds and bodies of victims, but to their souls.

That's why the United States, under the leadership of Congress and President Bush, is taking strong action, in cooperation with other nations, to end human trafficking. We have 11 U.S. government agencies executing strategic anti-trafficking in persons plans through the President's Interagency Task Force on Trafficking in Persons. The U.S. devoted more than $70 million in the last fiscal year to anti-trafficking programs abroad to prevent trafficking, protect victims, and prosecute traffickers. We issue the most comprehensive report on trafficking in persons in an effort to stimulate greater government action around the world, and we are aggressively stepping up prosecution and public education efforts here at home.

It is from a worldwide perspective, however, that I am here to speak with you. Without a doubt, there are many things we still are striving to understand about this criminal phenomenon known as human trafficking. But as we get further into our research and examine trends, we certainly are identifying common threads that bind disparate trafficking scenarios together.

*Vulnerability of victims*

First, we know that in a vast majority of human trafficking cases, the victims are from vulnerable populations. Traffickers prey on those they deem easier targets: those with little or no financial means who might be lured by promises of food, money, and shelter; innocent children who have no means of physically defending themselves; and people who have been given few or no educational opportunities. In many cases, traffickers rely on psychological coercion to take advantage of vulnerable people, but they also use physical force to profit in human misery. Our most recent estimates reveal that 80 percent of trafficking victims worldwide are female and 50 percent are children.

*Deception as a key tool of traffickers*

Second, through data collection and research conducted as part of our preparation of the congressionally mandated "Trafficking in Persons Report," we find that most traffickers offer victims false promises of better lives. Taking advantage of the financial vulnerability I just mentioned, human traffickers deceive victims with non-existent job opportunities, financial windfall, and much improved living conditions. Victims often believe these lies because they have seen glimpses of other cultures in the media or have heard supposed "success stories" from others who have left the country to pursue their dreams. Sadly, deception is even sometimes used by people they trust who get money for signing friends or relatives up for human trafficking situations.

*Corruption as a contributing factor*

A third thread we have identified in the fight against human trafficking is the role of systemic corruption, which provides valuable cover for those who trade in people. Where governments are not trusted and not perceived as upholding justice, citizens lose confidence in their ability to thrive in those nations. They become more desperate and willing to take unwise risks, making them more prone to trafficking schemes. Furthermore, when they get in difficult or potentially criminal situations, victims fear, rather than seek out, government intervention. This cycle of corruption and distrust fuels economic instability, destroys confidence in the legal system, and undermines the rule of law.

So how do vulnerability, deception, and corruption relate to a potential link between marriage brokering and human trafficking?

Traffickers rely on the vulnerable, and taking a woman out of her community, transporting her from her country, and making her dependent on a foreign man in a foreign land makes her ripe for exploitation.

Many women in less developed countries long for a move to a more developed country where life is thought to be easier. One way "out" for women in economically depressed communities is to marry citizens of more developed countries. And where governments offer no civil protections, this option leaves women with little information about their prospective marriage matches and whether they have been married before, have criminal records, etc.

Traffickers are documented to have used offers of marriage to recruit women for the sex trade and for forced labor. From rural villages in Asia to slums in major South American cities, women are deceived into leaving their homes and traveling across international borders in the hopes of marrying men who can provide them better lives. This vulnerability of disadvantaged women is well known to traffickers.

Some human traffickers recruit victims through direct offers of marriages, negotiating directly with the woman or her family for a promise of marriage, after which she is delivered to a brothel or a sweatshop by the "husband," who is rewarded with a cash payment from the brothel keeper or sweatshop manager for the delivery of his slave.

This was the case with a woman I met in Asia in February. Pou was 17 when a man came to her village and arranged through her sister to marry her. Shortly after the marriage, the man took Pou to a fishing village and sold her to a brothel. After years of abuse and torment, Pou was released by the brothel. Today her body is ravaged by disease, and this woman in her 20s looks decades older than her real age. Yet she wants her story told.

To further illustrate the prevalence of this scenario, I'd like to tell you about the effort of a non-government organization in one Asian community. The NGO began a program to prevent human trafficking by taking Polaroid photographs of each man who comes to a particular community to take a bride. These photos are then used to identify men who return to the community for brides multiple times, revealing some men to be traffickers who have no interest in real marriages to the women they claim to be picking up as brides.

Other villains in this trade, however, use more organized mechanisms for deceiving women with offers of marriage. We believe marriage brokers—legal brokers who, for a fee, introduce prospective brides to wealthier foreign men—are used to facilitate trafficking in persons. Documenting this trend, however, is not easy.

NGOs and other sources provide anecdotal evidence of this connection. Recent reports reveal trafficking of women from Vietnam to Taiwan in which many Vietnamese women are married legally to Taiwanese men whom they do not know until they are transported to Taiwan. In these cases, marriage brokers appear to be used—advertising and recruiting women seeking a foreign marriage as a means to improve their lives, only to be forced into sexual servitude in brothels in Taiwan.

While the examples presented here deal with Asia, they are stories repeated around the world. It is important to note that this is a worldwide phenomenon that likely touches many countries and every continent.

The potential for similar trafficking of foreign women to the United States using ostensibly legal and legitimate marriage brokers is real and serious. I applaud your efforts, Mr. Chairman, Senator Cantwell's efforts, and the actions of others to tighten oversight of marriage brokers operating in the United States in order to prevent the abuse of vulnerable women and children.

I am now happy to take your questions.

Senator BROWNBACK. Thank you, Director Miller, and thank you for your comments on this.

I have been around this debate now from the beginning of it. The late Senator Wellstone and I worked and pulled and pushed on this together. I appreciate your maturing the information because, at first, we did not know the nature of what all we were really dealing with. We just kept running into it anecdotally and then some information was coming forward, but we were not really sure about it. Now as this is coming in more sharp relief, we can get a much better picture of the size and scale of what all we are dealing with, and it is profound. And the different ways it is done and conducted I think is important for us to be able to get that out and to address those various avenues, whether it is through some sort of false marriage proposals or mail order bride type proposals. I think that is important to do.

Paul and I both looked at this and said this is one of the dark clouds of the globalization, where you get in a world that opens up and people can travel more freely and the fall of the wall and communism and people are able to move. But this has been one of the dark sides of it, and we really have to continue to be real vigilant. And you have done a great job of doing that.

Thanks for being here with us today.

Mr. MILLER. Thank you, Mr. Chairman.

Senator BROWNBACK. Our third panel is a panel of experts on this topic. Ms. Michele A. Clark, co-director of the Protection Project of the Foreign Policy Institute for Johns Hopkins University, a person who knows this topic very well on trafficking: Dr. Donna Hughes, professor, Women's Studies Program, University of Rhode Island; and Ms. Suzanne Jackson, associate professor of Clinical Law at George Washington University Law School here in Washington, DC.

Ladies, your full statements will be placed into the record, so you are free to summarize the points that you would like to make. I would like, if you could, to stay around 5 minutes so we could have some time for questioning afterwards. Unfortunately, because of time constraints, we need to get this hearing done in an hour.

So, Ms. Clark, thank you very much for being with us. I look forward to your presentation.

## STATEMENT OF MICHELE A. CLARK, CO-DIRECTOR, PROTECTION PROJECT OF THE FOREIGN POLICY INSTITUTE, JOHNS HOPKINS UNIVERSITY

Ms. CLARK. It is my pleasure, Mr. Chairman. I thank you very much for the opportunity to be here today and would like to begin by thanking you and acknowledging your tremendous contribution in the war against modern-day slavery. You have been a dear friend of many of ours in this room and in other areas, and we thank you for your continued commitment.

I would also like to acknowledge the role of other government agencies in this, our friend John Miller at the trafficking office and his excellent staff, as well as extremely dedicated people at the Department of Labor, HHS, United States Agency for International Development, and our Department of Justice, all whose efforts are contributing on a daily basis to eradicating trafficking.

I also have to acknowledge that without good research assistants, I could not do my job. I have a wonderful researcher named Anna Koppel. I would like to give her credit for her tremendous work in helping us.

We have heard already from Senator Cantwell and from Mr. Miller the story of abuse that takes place in this industry. We have heard of the case of Mrs. King. We have heard of the murder committed by Mr. Blackwell. We know the story of Alla Barney, a 26-year-old Ukrainian mail order bride who was stabbed to death by her own husband, Lester Barney, 58, after she obtained a restraining order against him and temporary custody of their son on allegations of abuse.

I could continue the stories, and I am sure we will hear many more, but what stymies me, Senator, as I listen to this, is how do we get to this point. What has created such a monster that an industry, mail order brides, which has a relatively long history, certainly in American social culture and history, and the Internet, which is destined to provide us with some good and make our lives easier, have contributed to the creation of the contemporary Hydra. It seems that every time we try to knock off one head, another evil head emerges to reveal how evil this practice particularly is. So I would like in my testimony to talk about this a little bit, why this is happening and where the particular points of vulnerability are.

In countries around the world, we have seen how economic and social collapse, civil war, and natural disasters have been used as vehicles to deceive, entrap, and enslave vulnerable women and children into lives of cruel exploitation. Traffickers capitalize on desperation and need, as do the mail order bride industries. They also exploit normal desires, and this is important to realize. They exploit normal desires for a better life, for hope, for the fulfillment of dreams. Many women who enter into a contract with an international matchmaking organization, especially in the booming former Soviet Union industry, are women with educations, but what they see is an opportunity for something that perhaps is more resembling a Western relationship, and when faced with the high rates of domestic violence and abuse on their own home front, they find this rather appealing. In addition, they are rather lavishly and romantically wooed. Our colleagues at the Taheri Justice Center have done some good research on this very matter. So it is not surprising that the industry of marriage should become a vehicle for exploitation, and nor should it be surprising that the Internet, because of its immediacy, because of promises of anonymity and lack of accountability, should become the vehicle of choice.

Now, at the earliest inception, matchmaking institutions, even the picture bride industry, included the involvement of parties that knew the groom and/or the bride personally. So one other answer to the question of why women enter into these relationships is that in many countries the idea of the matchmaker of song and fame is actually an acceptable practice. Usually, however, this matchmaker was someone known to the women, known to the husbands, known to the families, and was a common denominator. Now the "matchmaker, matchmaker, make me a match" has been replaced by an impersonal, anonymous, and profit-seeking Web-based mechanism.

While some matchmaking organizations take a personal approach to their business, the vast majority of mail order bride matches now happen through the mediation of Internet-based matchmaking organizations where connections occur in bulk, catalogs contain hundreds or thousands of profiles of available brides, and where matchmakers rarely have personal clients.

Here is an interesting point. With the spread of the Internet, anyone with a Web connection can now run a matchmaking business. The industry has ballooned greatly in recent years and has become very commercial. Many on-line mail order bride Web sites have taken a pure merchandising approach to their matchmaking, one with which any of us who go onto a catalog, a book site are familiar with. Just as we find buttons that say "browse," "select," "proceed to checkout," these same setups are visible on matchmaking organizations.

In the written testimony provided to the committee, as well on the table, we have provided an illustration of what one such Web site, Alena Russian Bride Marriage Agency, looks like. You have a shopping cart. Your order list. An instruction to "preview your order list with photos." Another icon tells you to "proceed to checkout." Underneath this are the words, "Search our catalog to find your future Russian wife. 100 percent satisfaction guaranty or money back. No questions." With the reduction of women to such a commodity very little different from a sweater, a sweatshirt, or a car part that I would buy, it is no wonder that the attitude that continues in a relationship continues to be one of ownership.

Just before I close, let me read you two quotes. One is from a Filipina woman who ended up in a relationship with a man through a site called Intimate Submissives. This man said: "I need to find myself a nice submissive young lady who wants and needs to have me control her, teaching a young woman to submit fully to my wishes. If my wife does not obey me, I am perfectly willing to punish her in whatever way I think is my right." And because satisfaction is guaranteed, this gentleman feels he has the license to operate in such a way.

In a less gruesome but still telling quote, a young American potential groom states about women in Ukraine: "The girls here, their values and ethics are like American girls back in the 1950s. They are willing to put their family first, their man first, instead of themselves."

And to sum it up, an illuminating commentary quoted on A Foreign Affair, a Web site for citing Maxim Magazine, which says why the industry beats the real world. "Unless you work for the United Nations, your odds of being introduced to this many foreign women are a zillion to one. And with a round-trip ticket to Moscow running some $1,500, shelling out $10 for one woman's address is a hell of a lot more cost-efficient. Bonus: fewer tedious discussions about the 'relationship' when your fiancée's vocabulary is limited to yes, sex, and green card."

Mr. Chairman, thank you for your consideration, and I look forward to answering any questions you might have.

[The prepared statement of Ms. Clark follows:]

PREPARED STATEMENT OF MICHELE A. CLARK

MAIL-ORDER BRIDES: EXPLOITED DREAMS

Mr. Chairman, Members of the Committee:

It is an honor to be here before you today. My name is Michele Clark, and I am the codirector of the Protection Project, a human rights research institute located at the Johns Hopkins University School of Advanced International Studies. For the past seven years, we have focused on documenting and analyzing the complex dimensions of human trafficking both in the United States and in countries around the world. We have worked with Members of Congress, U.S. Government agencies and American NGOs, as well as representatives of foreign governments and NGOs to develop sound policy and practice in the war against trafficking and to conduct training, here and overseas, on the provision of services to victims of trafficking, drafting anti-trafficking legislation, and identifying victims of trafficking.

Mr. Brownback, I would like to acknowledge your championship of this issue and your continuing, courageous efforts to end modern day slavery. On behalf of victims of trafficking in Central and South America, in the Middle East, in Eastern and Western Europe, in Africa and Southeast Asia, I would like to thank you for your commitment to the freedom of these men and women, too many of them children. As evidenced by the most recent Trafficking in Persons Report, documenting the status of human trafficking in 140 countries around the world, released in June by Mr. Miller and his extremely capable staff at the Trafficking in Persons Office, we have seen that significant progress has been made, and that the efforts of the U.S. Government agencies involved in this battle, including the Departments of Justice, Health and Human Services, Labor, State and USAID are bearing fruit. We also recognize that we still have a long way to go.

Those of us who have been involved in the war against trafficking for a number of years have learned many important lessons which assist us in honing our own efforts to end modern day slavery. One lesson in particular has been the creativity and ingenuity of traffickers to adapt to different social, economic and political trends. Allow me to provide you with a few examples:

When Soviet Jews began leaving Russia en masse for Israel in the early 1990s, traffickers rightly assumed that the entrance into the country of a few thousand illegal women for the purposes of being forced into the brothels of Tel Aviv, Jerusalem and Haifa would pass unnoticed, given the large numbers of legal immigrants and the limited resources to process all newcomers. They were right, and the trade in women remained fairly covert until the mid nineties.

When the numbers of Chinese workers seeking to obtain illegal entry into the United States began to grow, smugglers started charging exorbitant fees for passage to California or New York. Instead of a family being able to scrape together the full fare, those seeking entry would pay a portion of their transportation up front and agree to pay the balance upon their arrival in the United States. In order to do this, they signed contracts which bound them to their employers until the debt was paid, turning a smuggling operation into a crime of human trafficking.

In countries around the world, we see how economic and social collapse, civil war and natural disasters have been used as vehicles to deceive, entrap and enslave vulnerable women and children into lives of cruel exploitation. Traffickers capitalize on desperation and need; they also exploit normal desires for a better life, for hope, for the fulfillment of dreams.

So it is not surprising that the industry of marriage should become a vehicle for exploitation. Nor is it surprising that the Internet, because of its immediacy, promises of anonymity and lack of accountability, should become the vehicle of choice for this exploitation to take place.

*Overview of the Industry*

The practice of pre-arranged marriages, or mail-order brides, conducted through a third party, is not new to the United States, and can be documented as far back as the Revolutionary War. The practice was further developed during the California Gold Rush and the pioneer move west when pictures of available women were distributed to men in isolated regions. At times the mail-order bride industry filled deeply human needs. Following the Armenian Genocide, matchmaking organizations facilitated marriages of "picture brides," or women displaced as a result of the Genocide, enabling them to make connections with other Armenians in different parts of the world, notably Canada. In this instance, the service enabled members of a tragically dispersed community to find one another and reestablish ties with members of their own ethnic group.

In the early nineteen nineties, the Internet replaced the picture catalogues and began posting photographs as well as profiles of young women interested in finding a foreign spouse, facilitating communication and providing men with access to a larger pool of applicants. Previously dominated by women from Southeast Asia (especially the Philippines), the rise of the Internet, coinciding with the fall of the former Soviet Union and the subsequent economic collapse which plunged many families into desperate economic conditions, contributed to the meteoric rise of the Russian mail-order bride industry.

*How Large Is the Industry Today?*

The simplest Google search for "mail-order brides" yields a minimum of 500,000 Web page entries with names such as "The Natasha Club," "Brides4U," "Plant-Love," "Goodwife," and "LoveMe." Out of the first twenty entries on the Google search, only one entry deals with the possibility of abuse and negative outcomes of matches arranged on line. The majority of the entries are dedicated to Eastern European, Latina and Asian women profiled as mail-order brides looking for husbands. On an average Google page, firms offering Russian brides comprise about 30 percent of all advertisements.

Several Sites advertise themselves as warehouses. The "Mail-Order Bride Warehouse," available at *www.goodwife.com,* provides a good indicator of the popularity of the international match-making industry, which boasts 12,804,307 hits since August 31, 1997.

As of June 2004, we were able to find over 400 Web sites based in the U.S. offering international marriage broker services; this number does not include the number of firms operating overseas. It is estimated that outside of the U.S., there are over 500 Web sites operating in the former Soviet Union alone, with more than 62,000 Russian and 30,000 Ukrainian women listed in their rosters.

The mail-order bride industry is largely unregulated. Web-based companies appear and disappear everyday. The international on-line matchmaking business appears to be thriving largely because of increased Internet use worldwide, low overhead and start-up costs, and the seemingly endless supply of eligible foreign women. Today, any man with Internet access, an electronic photo (even ten years old) and a credit card number can shop.

*Who Are the Brides and Where Do They Come From?*

In 2002, 18,621 former fiancées were adjusted to permanent residence status in the United States. Out of that number, 4,739 were from Europe (1,476 from Russia and 861 from Ukraine); 9,358 were from Asia (1,361 from China; 2,392 from the Philippines, 2,418 from Vietnam); and 966 were from South America (346 from Brazil, 301 from Colombia).[1]

The mail-order bride trade follows traditional trafficking patterns, with brides coming from the former Soviet Union countries, Asia and Latin America, and the clients coming from the West (including Europe and North America). The nationalities most represented in the mail-order bride industry are from Eastern Europe (with a strong emphasis on Russia and Ukraine), Asia (specifically the Philippines, China, Vietnam and Thailand), and Latin America (most prominently represented by Colombia, Brazil and Costa Rica).

Clients are from the U.S., Canada, Europe (notably Germany, Sweden and Norway), and Japan.

*A Legitimate Industry Goes Sour—From Legitimate Practice to Exploitation and Abuse*

While the mail-order bride industry is not in itself an illegitimate business, it is characterized by several important features which render it susceptible to exploitative practices. Without appropriate safeguard regulations, the industry will continue to be ripe for exploitation by unscrupulous business owners. Because it is a commercial enterprise, it favors the interests of the paying clients, usually men, over the interests of the brides.

*Commercialization of the Mail-Order Bride Industry*

At their earliest inception, most matchmaking institutions, even the picture bride industry, included the involvement of parties that knew the groom and/or the bride personally. The "matchmaker" of song and movies was a regular fixture in many cultures. The mail-order bride industry as it has developed today is a largely impersonal, multi-million dollar business where a profit-based corporation now fills the role of the middleman. While some matchmaking organizations still take a personal approach to their business, the vast majority of mail-order bride matches now take place through the mediation of Internet-based matchmaking organizations, where connections occur in bulk, catalogs contain hundreds or thousands of profiles of available brides, and where matchmakers rarely have personal contact with their clients. With the spread of the Internet, anyone with a Web connection is now able to run a matchmaking business. The industry has thus ballooned greatly in recent years, and has become more commercial. Many online mail-order bride Web sites have taken a Web-based merchandising approach to their matchmaking, one in which the male clients are taken through a process of "Browse, Select, Proceed to Checkout." Some organizations, such as Alena Russian Brides Marriage Agency, even use computer icons similar to those found on Internet catalogue sites, complete with pictures of shopping carts and money back guarantees:

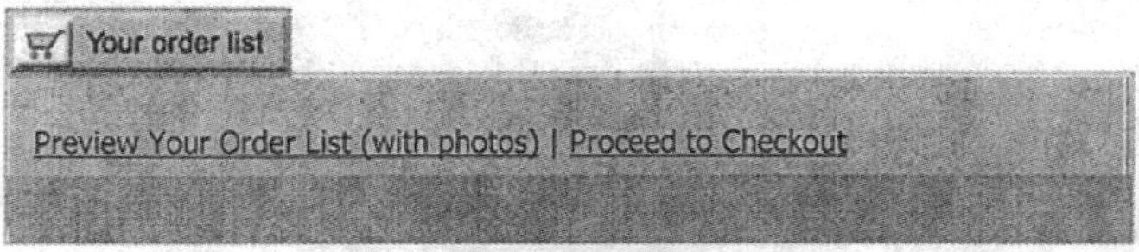


Search our catalog **to find your future Russian wife. 100% Satisfaction Guaranty or money back. No questions.**[2]

A Foreign Affair, at the *www.loveme.com* Web site, reprints an informational piece with permission of Maxim magazine, which provides another type of illustrative description of the contemporary mail-order bride industry: "It's a snap to narrow the field. Though your typical guy won't admit it, 20,000 women are more than he can handle. *Luckily, AFA* [A Foreign Affair] *has made searching its voluminous database as easy as ordering a pizza.*[3] As the mail-order bride industry becomes an increasingly commercial affair, this leads the clients to view marriage with a foreign woman as a commercial transaction, one characterized by a "satisfaction guaranteed, or your money back approach." Further, if the client is not satisfied with the provided product, he can always "return and exchange" his bride, which some men have done with disastrous consequences. In the famous Anastasia King case, Indle G. King Jr. was convicted in September 2002 for the first-degree murder of his *second* mail-order bride. According to King's testimony, he had not been satisfied with his first "product."[4] He then righted that wrong by taking revenge on his second try.

Money-back guarantees usually mean that, if a client does not find a satisfactory match within a specified time, he is entitled to a refund of his money. Within this framework, matchmaking organizations have little incentive to seek out information from their male clients as to their potentially negative personal histories including criminal records and marital history. In the interest of profit, what matters is the quantity of the matches being made by the matchmaking organization rather than the quality of the matches made.

*Commercial Stereotyping in the Mail-Order Bride Industry*

Matchmaking organizations build their business by taking advantage of and marketing cultural stereotypes. The danger with these stereotypes stems from their inherent flaws in describing reality and the possible consequences of such misrepresentations. In relationships like those of the mail-order bride variety, where partners know very little about each other, stereotypes can play a destructive role, potentially leading to abuse. Many matchmaking Web sites advertise their mail-order brides (implicitly, or in some cases, explicitly) as submissive, docile, faithful and loving domesticated wives who are looking to build a traditional, old fashioned home in which they will cater to their man. It is not unlikely that the men who choose to pursue the search for a wife through the mail-order bride path might be looking for just such a woman. It is also likely that a man who is seeking out a submissive woman is not seeking an equal partnership, but rather a relationship of dominance and control.[5] It is further likely that a man who marries a bride from a mail-order match will expect her to fit this stereotype. However, stereotypes are unlikely to reflect the reality of the personalities of even a minority of the women which they advertise. It then becomes likely that if a wife turns out not to "live up" to the advertised standard, the husband, who was seeking control in a relationship, might turn to abuse in order to force the wife to live up to that standard. While little research has been done to investigate this issue, the little information available does point to the fact that men seeking mail-order brides might indeed be searching for the stereotyped women. Even more poignantly, the businesses of mail-order brides would not be marketing a stereotype for which there is little demand. A Filipina quotes a letter which she has received from an interested man who found her photo through the "Intimate Submissives Web site": ". . . I need to find myself a nice submissive young lady who wants and needs to have me control . . . teaching a young woman to submit fully to my wishes . . . If my wife does not obey me, I am perfectly willing to punish her in whatever way I think is right . . ."[6] In a less gruesome, but still telling quote, a young American potential groom states about women in Ukraine "The girls here, their values and ethics are like American girls back in the 195Os, they're willing to put their family first, to put their man first instead of themselves."[7] And to sum it up, an illuminating commentary quoted on A Foreign Affair's Web site from Maxim Magazine: "Why it [Mail-order Bride Industry] beats the real world: 'Unless you work for the United Nations, your odds of being introduced to this many foreign women are a zillion to one. And with a round-trip ticket to Moscow running some $1,500, shelling out $10 for one woman's address is a hell of a lot more cost-efficient. Bonus: fewer tedious discussions about the "relationship" when your fiancée's vocabulary is limited to yes, sex, and green card.'"[8]

*Inherent Bias Against the Mail-Order Bride: Exploitation of Conditions of Vulnerability*

As the mail-order bride industry is first and foremost a business, the customer's satisfaction is logically the central concern. Because the paying clients are male, the bride is reduced to the condition of commodity. Protective mechanisms exist to safeguard the potential husbands, but not the potential brides. The mail-order brides face conditions of vulnerability prior to marriage with their potential grooms, during the matchmaking process, and after the marriage takes place.

*Informational Vulnerability*

A significant imbalance leading to a condition of vulnerability concerns the information about partners available to prospective brides and grooms. Potential brides generally receive information which has been volunteered by the potential husband himself. While matchmaking organizations have incentive to provide their paying male clients with "quality" brides, the incentive is much smaller for providing the prospective brides with similar information about their possible husbands, especially considering the seemingly unrelenting supply of available brides. Matchmaking organizations commonly do not screen their male clients for past criminal records or records of domestic violence, abuse or restraining orders. According to Bob Burrows, the President of Cherry Blossoms, one of the longest-running and largest mail-order bride agencies in the United States, a "serial murderer could write to [Cherry Blossoms] and there's no screening done."[9] While background checks on the brides are sometimes provided to the potential husbands to minimize the chances of the foreign woman "swindling" the male clients, the same background checks are not done about the potential husbands to minimize chances of abuse against the brides. The industry therefore almost en masse ignores the potential repercussions of these marriages on the women, while focusing squarely on the potential repercussions of the marriages on the men, leaving the brides to be in a more vulnerable position than the grooms.

*Economic Vulnerability*

Most matchmaking organizations make their profits from the arrangement of marriages between two worlds—the first and the third. Similar to the trafficking in persons industry, husbands tend to come from wealthy, stable economies, while the brides originate from economically unstable or vulnerable environments. Additionally, the mail-order brides are in conditions of economic vulnerability before and after their marriage to their first-world husbands. Most women search for a husband abroad out of economic need, as demonstrated by the one-way direction of the marriages—no Web sites exist advertising American or German women as mail-order brides in El Salvador or the Ukraine, for example. However, when these brides find themselves married in the first world, they are dependent economically on their husbands especially in the early days of their lives in a new country. They thus continue to face economic vulnerability and dependency until the time comes when they are able to support themselves financially.

*Cultural Vulnerability*

An additional bias stems from the fact that the brides enter a foreign country, a foreign culture, and a foreign community, in which few of them have any networks of support other than the husband—the matchmaking agencies tend not to stay involved in the future of a marriage. The husband, who has brought a wife into his natural environment, is by default in his comfort zone, while the wife is vulnerable to the intricacies of a culture she is not familiar with, often without the knowledge of the language. She is again dependent in many ways on the husband until she begins to navigate the culture herself.

*Legal Vulnerability*

Additionally, because the brides are usually from a foreign country, they are in a legally vulnerable status, dependent on their newly found husbands for continued legal presence in their new homes. In the United States, a woman arriving on a fiancée visa is to be married to her proposed fiancée within 90 days of entry (there is no legal way to extend this limit), or she is to face deportation. Upon marriage, she is granted a conditional resident status, which is again dependent on her husband, as applications are filed jointly. Again, before the expiration of the continued status, the wife and the husband must appear in court together to request removal of conditionality. Divorce cannot be an option for two years, otherwise the wife loses her immigrant status. The bride is therefore continuously placed at the mercy of her husband and lives under the constant threat of possible deportation.[10] While recent laws have been enacted to allow immigrant women who have suffered abuse at the hands of their American husbands to file alone for permanent residence, few women are informed of this law. In 1996 matchmaking organizations were required by law to disclose information about immigration laws to its brides or pay $20,000 fines, but it is not clear how well-enforced this law has been. The legal bias is therefore also in favor of the men, and not the brides.

*Lack of Industry Regulation*

The low start-up costs and the ease of creating a matchmaking organization online create conditions that are ripe for abusive practices. Few standards exist for the operation of these agencies other than the U.S. imposed fine for failure to disclose immigration information. For example, in a rare effort of the mail-order bride industry to self-regulate, matchmaking agencies which market brides through catalogs as well as over the Internet, claim that they refrain from sending catalogs to prison addresses. However, some journalists have found references to access to catalogs within the prison system.[11] The lack of regulation of the industry leaves it open to a wide array of potential criminal violations, the most important being the trafficking in persons for sex and labor under the guise of mail-order marriages, the ease of entry of organized crime into such business, and the recruitment of minors as potential mail-order brides, as well as the organization of sex tours which could involve minors under the guise of "romance tours." Nongovernmental organizations have linked matchmaking organizations based in Russia with Russian organized crime, and romance tours have been observed to serve as fronts for high-level prostitution rings.[12] Marie Claire Belleau, in "Mail-order Brides in a Global World," quotes an interview with a Canadian Social Worker in a shelter for immigrant women who have experienced spousal abuse, who states that "In the worst case scenario, the First World Husband assumes the role of a pimp, who takes away the bride's passport and forces her into prostitution. At one extreme, the pimp may go so far as to undertake serial sponsorships of immigrant women to supply new recruits for prostitution rings. If this is the case, he will hold the bride in debt bondage because he paid for her to immigrate to North America, and then force her to participate in slavery-like practices in order to obtain her freedom." Without regulation, Web-based matchmaking organizations can easily recruit women into prostitution rings. Some may charge potential brides exorbitant fees for matching them up with a husband, and then place them in debt bondage. The Council of Europe has recently pointed to the lack of regulation of the mail-order bride industry in its April 2004 Report on "Domestic Slavery: Servitude, Au Pairs and Mail-order Brides," and called for some type of regulation. The Council of Europe stated that "it is in the interest of the more serious agencies to accept some type of regulation . . . the persons responsible for a site should be clearly identifiable, users of the site should be forced to identify themselves, marriages should be kept track of, and an emergency contact number should be provided for when things go wrong. Agencies should also do a background check on the prospective bridegroom to check for a criminal record (e.g. domestic violence or procurement) when couples come close to marriage." Further, the Council of Europe recommended considering including "mail-order brides" in the scope of its draft convention against trafficking in human beings, and the development of an accreditation system for matchmaking agencies which would commit them to adherence to a number of agreed upon minimum standards which would serve to protect the potential mail-order brides.

Regulation is urgently needed to eliminate the existing biases that favor the male clients and to counter with protective regulation the conditions of vulnerability mail-order brides find themselves in within the contemporary context of the mail-order bride industry.

*Documentation of Abuse*

*Physical Abuse:* Ngan, a twenty-one year old Filipina came to the United States having married a U.S. citizen through an international matchmaking organzation. She endured repeated physical assaults at the hands of her husband who had decided that he had not receive the picture bride that he had ordered. Frightened in the beginning, Ngan did not report what had happened to her. As the violence increased, Ngan's neighbors rescued her, and from the hospital she was placed in a shelter for battered Asian women.[14]

*Physical Abuse, Forced Motherhood and Threats of Deportation:* In a story of forced motherhood, Raco, a twenty-four year old Filipina, married a U.S. citizen, who had corresponded with her romantically for ten years. Soon after her marriage, Raco began to be severely beaten by her husband. Because she did not want to bear children immediately, the assaults against her became more severe. When Raco did become pregnant, she was threatened by her husband who said that he would not sponsor her permanent residence if she did not carry the child to term. She finally fled to a shelter, after the beatings continued to intensify even when she decided to keep the child.[15]

*Physical Abuse, Threats of Deportation, Restriction of Movement and Murder:* In the most famous mail order bride abuse case, Anastasia King from Kyrgyzstan married Ingle King, Jr., who strangled her to death in September 2000. It has been reported that in her diaries, Anastasia wrote that she was sexually and physically assaulted by King, that he withheld her college tuition, restricted her freedom of movement, and threatened her with deportation and death.[16]

*Physical Abuse and Murder:* Alla Barney, a twenty-six year old Ukrainian mail order bride was stabbed to death by her husband, Lester S. "Stuart" Barney, 58, after she had obtained a restraining order against him and temporary custody of their son on allegations of abuse. Alla had met Barney through an online mail order bride service.[17]

*Physical Abuse and Murder:* After a year long courtship, Susana Remerata, a Filipina, married Timothy Blackwell, who had found her on the Asian Encounters Web site. After their wedding in the Philippines, Blackwell became abusive and attempted to choke Susana on several occasions. Susana had filed for divorce, but before the proceedings were set to begin, Blackwell shot and murdered Susana and her unborn child in a Seattle Courthouse.[18]

*Sexual Abuse of a Child, Forced Labor:* Norman H. McDonald pled guilty to sexually abusing his Ukrainian mail order wife's daughter since the age of 3. McDonald had also forced his wife to hold several.jobs.[19]

*Physical Abuse, Failure to Provide Immigration Information:* Nataliya Fox, a Russian who came to the United States on a K-1 visa, has recently filed a lawsuit against Encounters International, a long-standing matchmaking service in Maryland. Nataliya was originally set to marry a Virginian whom she had met through Encounters, but upon the failure of that marriage, Encounters set her up with another match, James Fox. Nataliya and James were married within the month, however Nataliya was severely assaulted by James while she was breastfeeding their newborn daughter. A few months prior to that incident, Nataliya had informed Encounters that her husband had hit her. Nataliya's lawsuit charges Encounters with failing to have run a background check on her husband's previous history (which includes an accusation from a former fiancée of his attempt to strangle her to death) and with failing to provide her with the legally required immigration information about her ability to self-petition for permanent residence as a battered immigrant woman. James Fox is currently married to another mail-order bride.[20]

Mr. Chairman, members of the committee, on behalf of these women, and the thousands more whose stories we never hear about but who endure lives of horrible abuse, we urge you to take aggressive action to protect these women who, in many cases, have done nothing more than tried to follow their dreams.

Thank you for your time.

NOTES

[1] USCIS 2002 Yearbook of Immigration Statistics, accessed July 9, 2004 at http://uscis.gov/graphics/shared/aboutus/statistics/IMM02yrbk/IMM2002.pdf.

[2] Picture and quote from Alena Russian Bride Marriage Agency, accessed July 9, 2004 at http://www.alena-marriage-agency.com/.

[3] A Foreign Affair, accessed July 10, 2004 at, http://www.loveme.com/information/maxim.shtml.

[4] David Fisher, "Indle King Found Guilty of Killing Mail-Order Bride," *Seattle Post-Intelligence Reporter,* February 22,2002.

[5] Robert J. Scholes, PhD, "The 'Mail-Order Bride' Industry and Its Impact on U.S. Immigration," accessed July 9, 2004 at http://uscis.gov/graphics/aboutus/repsstudies/Mobappa.htm, quoting Glodava, Mila and Richard Onizuka, "Mail Order Brides: Women for Sale," 1994.

[6] Quote from Media Rights, synopsis of "Say I Do 'Mail-Order Brides,'" accessed July 10, 2004 at http://www.mediarights.org/search/fil_detailphp?ffl_id=06229.

[7] Sara Rainsford, "Romance Tourists' Head East," *BBC News,* July 9, 2002.

[8] A Foreign Affair, accessed July 10, 2004 at, http://www.loveme.com/information/maxim.shtm1.

[9] Quote from Vanessa B.M. Vergara, "Abusive Mail-Order Marriage and the Thirteenth Amendment," Northwestern University Law Review, Summer 2000.
[10] Vanessa B.M. Vergara, "Abusive Mail-Order Marriage and the Thirteenth Amendment," Northwestern University Law Review, Summer 2000.
[11] Lena H. Sun, "The Search for Miss Right Takes a Turn Toward Russia," *The Washington Post,* March 8, 1998.
[12] See, for example, "Crime and Servitude: An Expose of the Traffic in Women for Prostitution from the Newly Independent States," Global Survival Network, 1997.
[13] Marie-Claire Belleau, "Mail-Order Brides in a Global World," Albany Law Review, 2003.
[14] Michelle J. Anderson, "A License to Abuse: The Impact of Conditional Status on Female Immigrants," From the Web site, Mail Order Brides and the Abuse of Immigrant Women, synopsis of by Anderson, Michelle J., accessed on July 11, 2004 at *http://nostatusquo.com/ACLU/Anderson/brides/pgl.html.*
[15] Michelle J. Anderson, "A License to Abuse: The Impact of Conditional Status on Female Immigrants," from the Web site, Mail Order Brides and the Abuse of Immigrant Women, synopsis of by Anderson, Michelle J., accessed on July 11, 2004 at *http://nostatusguo.com/ACLU/Anderson/brides/pgl.html.*
[16] Mae Bunagan, "Cash on Delivery," accessed on July 12, 2004 at *http://www.digitas.Harvard.edu/-perspy/issues/2002/nov/mae.html.*
[17] Troy Graham and Joseph A. Gambardello, "Police say Husband Killed His 'Mail-Order' Wife," The Inquirer, October 1, 2003. Accessed on July 12, 2004 at http://www.philly.com/mld/inquirer/news/local/6903067.htm?template=contentMo.
[18] Mae Bunagan, "Cash on Delivery," accessed on July 12, 2004 at *http://www.digitas.Harvard.edu/-perspy/issues/2002/nov/mae.html.*
[19] "Man Pleads guilty to Sex Abuse of Mail-Order Bride's Daughter," The Associated Press State and Local Wire, February 26, 2004.
[20] Nadya Labi, "The Business of Mail-Order Marriage," Legal Affair, accessed on July 12, 2004 at *http://www.legalaffairs.org/issues/January-February-2004/story*__labi__janfeb04.html.

Senator BROWNBACK. Well, it is a commodification, is it not? And it is a reduction of the human person to, as you say, an ownership type relationship and a degrading of the institution of marriage as well. I look forward to talking more about this.

Dr. Hughes.

## STATEMENT OF DONNA M. HUGHES, PH.D., PROFESSOR, WOMEN'S STUDIES PROGRAM, UNIVERSITY OF RHODE ISLAND

Dr. HUGHES. Good afternoon, Senator Brownback. It is very good to be here. Thank you for your leadership on these issues.

Each year thousands of women marry men they have met through marriage agencies. Driven by poverty, unemployment, and media images of Western lifestyles, women accept risky offers of marriage in hope of finding a better life. Although some women may find the love and opportunities they seek, many become victims of violence, sexual exploitation, and sex trafficking.

From examining the Web sites of marriage agencies, one can see that the women are marketed using sexual, racial, and ethnic stereotypes. The Web sites often include sexualized and semi-nude pictures of the women. The descriptions of the women claim that they are dedicated to a subservient role, solely oriented to pleasing men. The women are clearly being marketed to men who have been failures at establishing relationships with American women.

From my contacts and what we have heard earlier, we know that there are many documented cases of domestic violence involving women who have come here through marriage agencies, so I will not go into detail on that.

One of the things that I have documented through my research is that you can find underage girls and children on these marriage sites. One marriage agency offered women from Asia and Eastern Europe, and I have found blatant and subtle marketing of children for sexual purposes. One mail order bride agency from the Philippines had 19 girls aged 17 or younger. Several of the marriage agencies offering women from Russia, Ukraine, and Moldova have underage girls, ranging in age from 10 to 16 years of age, and listed them as looking for correspondents and as being future wives for men abroad.

There are also images and texts on marriage Web sites that have raised my suspicions that pedophiles may seek a vulnerable foreign wife with children as a way of having sexual access to children. For example, on Web sites you will see pictures of nude children in sort of seemingly innocent scenes like playing in the water in a fountain on a street, but when that is juxtaposed beside a mail order bride, then you can see that this would have interest for pedophiles.

These agencies are also specialized in women or girls from extremely vulnerable populations. One marriage agency that I documented operates from inside a Russian government social service agency that provides medical and social assistance to families with disabled children, single parent families, and other vulnerable layers of the population.

I also have documented marriage agencies offering introduction services and pornography of women with disabilities. The services are marketed to men with fetishes for missing limbs and congenital malformations. On the same agency site are photographs of orphans with disabilities, and the viewers are urged to adopt them. It would be very easy to see how predators could then get access to some very vulnerable women and children in this way.

Senator BROWNBACK. Do you have the listing of those sites that we could get a look at that?

Dr. HUGHES. Yes, I can give you all those details.

Senator BROWNBACK. Thank you.

Dr. HUGHES. In the 1990s, the Government of the Philippines banned the operation of marriage agencies and sex tour agencies. I do not know if there has ever been any prosecutions, but this new law did cause American operators of marriage agencies to move out of the Philippines. So I thought that was quite interesting. Although one American man continues to operate his marriage agency business from the United States, he has his own Filipina bride that he sends back in to contact women and recruit for his bride agency. But that is something for us to consider in the law. If the operation of a mail order bride agency is illegal in the Philippines, is it acceptable for a U.S. citizen to run a mail order bride agency with Filipino women in them? It is something to think about.

Many of the marriage agencies are part of larger commercial operations that offer a number of services, some of which are blatantly connected to the sex industry and involve the sexual exploitation of women. These multiple services include tours for men to meet the women, escort services, which is the euphemism for prostitution, modeling agencies, production of pornography, and travel agencies. A number of the marriage agencies' Web sites have links to pornographic Web sites and prostitution services. So it is easy to see how the intersections of these types of services would enable the sexual exploitation and trafficking of women.

It is easy to document how marriage agencies are involved in many forms of sexual exploitation. It is harder to prove involvement of these agencies in sex trafficking as the crime is defined by law, meaning that it is for purposes of the commercial exploitation and requires force, fraud, or coercion, although information from nongovernmental organizations working in these countries indicates that marriage agencies are involved in sex trafficking.

In St. Petersburg, I met with NGO representatives who said that marriage agencies are well organized businesses and protected by the political-business-criminal networks there, and as in other cities in Russia, the same people who own marriage agencies also own foreign travel and employment agencies, some of which are known to be traffickers.

When you think about a marriage agency, what it has is it has collected a pool of women, usually young, all indicated that they want to travel abroad or even to emigrate to go abroad. They tend to be single and able to move, and because of the information they collect, the agency now has extensive personal information about the women and their families and we know that that information is often used by traffickers then to coerce the women either into prostitution or staying in prostitution. So I think these agencies have really created a data base and a pool of women from which they can recruit likely victims.

Since I saw the light go off, I will stop there.

[The prepared statement of Dr. Hughes follows:]

PREPARED STATEMENT OF DONNA M. HUGHES, PH.D.

INTRODUCTION

Each year, thousands of women marry men they have met through marriage agencies. Driven by poverty, unemployment, and media images of Western lifestyles, women accept risky offers of marriage in hope of finding a better life. Although some women may find the romance and opportunities they seek, many become victims of violence, sexual exploitation, and sex trafficking.

In the 1980s, the mail-order-bride industry was small and brokers had to use printed catalogues or advertisements in the back of magazines to reach male customers. At that time, most of the women were recruited from Southeast Asia, particularly the Philippines and Thailand. In the early 1990s, two historical developments coincided to turn the mail-order bride market into a profitable, global business: the first was the collapse of the Soviet Union with the opening up of the borders for people, particularly women, to migrate, and the second was the digital information revolution of the Internet. The marriage brokers quickly moved to the Internet, which enabled them to expand and update their catalogue offerings and reach a global market of men quicker, easier, and less expensively.

Women who find partners through marriage agencies are probably at higher risk of becoming victims of violence and exploitation. From examining the Web sites of marriage agencies, one can see that the women are marketed using sexual, racial, and ethnic stereotypes. The Web sites often include sexualized and semi-nude pictures of the women. The descriptions of the women claim that they are dedicated to a subservient role, solely oriented to pleasing men. The women are clearly being marketed to men who have been failures at establishing relationships with American women. These men frequently blame their failed relationships on the character of American women. One agency said it was there to assist men in finding a "*loving and devoted*" woman whose "*views of relationships have not been ruined by unreasonable expectations.*" The advertisement on this agency's Web site said that these women were "*known to be pleasers and not competitors. They are feminine, NOT feminist.*" The following is another example of how Filipina women are marketed to American men:

> *It is less common to find an American woman who is interested in having a permanent marriage and family including a Husband. One easy way to see this is to look at ANY publication containing "personals" ads. The*

*women want someone who looks a certain way, and who has certain "social skills" such as dancing or clever conversation, someone who is interesting and exciting and seductive. Now go to my Web page (www.filipina.com) and look at what the girls say they want. It's all pretty simple, really. Over and over they state that they are happy to settle down FOREVER with a MAN who is willing to try to hold down a steady job and be a loving and understanding husband and father. This will get you exactly NO WHERE with an American girl!!!!!"*

From my contacts with domestic violence service providers, I have heard about numerous cases in which mail-order-brides ended up being battered, imprisoned, and sadistically sexually abused. There are documented cases of women being abused and/or murdered after marrying a man they met through a "marriage agency." In a well-publicized case, an American man was convicted of murdering his "mail-order-bride" from Kyrgyzstan. Previously, he had another Russian "mail-order-bride" before the wife he murdered. She had divorced him. The murderer said that the second wife would not be allowed to leave. There have been other cases of women who met American men through these agencies being seriously victimized and murdered.

DECEPTIVE PRACTICES

There have been documented cases of photographs being used on marriage agency Web sites without the women's knowledge or permission. In one case, a model, whose nude pictures appeared in an American online catalogue claimed that a photographer, for whom she had worked, sold the pictures without her permission to the marriage agency, along with her address and phone number. Upon investigation, the owner of a modelling agency that specialized in pornography admitted that he sold nude photographs of women to the marriage agency.

UNDERAGE CHILDREN ON MARRIAGE AGENCY WEB SITES

On marriage agency Web sites offering women from Asia and Eastern Europe, I found blatant and subtle marketing of children for sexual purposes.

One mail-order-bride agency from the Philippines had 19 girls aged 17 or younger. The following are descriptions of three of the youngest girls:

*ID # V001—Hazel; Age: 13; Height: 5′3″* (160 cm); Weight 95 lb. (43 kg); Children: none; Looking for a mate in age range 20-35. "I am now a freshman student at Saint Pius School. . . . I like outdoors having fun. I like to read magazine which is nice to me, especially to religious books. I sometime love to see a movie but not so . . . I really want to have a penpal who is loving, caring, honest, and family-oriented person. I am a marriage minded woman."

*ID # Y011—Eddy Mae; Age 14; Height: 5′2″* (157 cm); Weight 98 lb. (45 kg); Children: none; Looking for a mate in age range 18 to 25; "Currently, I'm a second year student of San Lorenzo Ruiz Academy of Polomolok; . . . My hobbies are writing, painting, and reading books. I love reading Valentine Romance and any love story pocket books. I like watching TV Patrol and Million Dollar Movies."

*ID # 1F12—Edrilyn; Age: 15, Height: 5′0″* (152 cm); Weight 95 lb. (43 kg); Children: none; Looking for a mate in age range 20 to 30. "I am working in my neighbor's house as a servant. At the same time I am studying at public school—as a sophomore student . . . I like playing (as I am a sportsminded), dancing, reading, writing. I am fond of reading magazines, especially Movie Star and Teen Star. I love to watch TV shows such as Bay Watch and Power Rangers, which is interesting too. I am self-supporting."

Several of the marriage agencies offering women from Russia, Ukraine and Moldova have underage girls listed as correspondents or future wives. A marriage agency in Chisinau, Moldova had a 14 year old girl; an agency located in Kherson, Ukraine had girls listed as being 15 and 16 years of age; another Ukrainian agency had contact addresses for girls aged 10, 14, and 16. And an agency in Odessa, Ukraine had contact information for several underage girls (aged 10, 12, 14 and 15) and a boy (aged 15).

One marriage agent offering women and girls from the Philippines complained on his Web site that the U.S. government will not allow his youngest brides on offer, who are under age 16, into the country. *"The service itself is not restricted by the American government, although they are real picky about getting your bride into the states—they won't give a visa to a bride under age sixteen."*

There are imagines and texts on marriage agency Web sites that have raised my suspicions that paedophiles may seek a foreign wife with children as a way to have sexual access to children. One Web site had photographs of naked children from the Philippines. Although the images were seemingly innocent—the pictures were of naked boys playing in a fountain—when juxtaposed alongside mail order brides, they conveyed a message that these children were available as well. Also, another marriage agency allowed viewers to sort the available women by whether or not they had children.

THE MARKETING OF EXTREMELY VULNERABLE POPULATIONS

There are a few marriage agencies that either specialize in or include women or girls from especially vulnerable populations.

One marriage agency operates from inside a Russian government social service agency that provides medial and social assistance to "families with disabled children, single-parent families, large families, and other vulnerable layers of the population." Services they provide include "psychological consulting both to children and adults," and "legal assistance to the women suffering domestic/sexual/societal" violence. The Web site appeared to be a typical marriage agency, and claimed that its purpose was to provide "assistance to the lonely people inside Russia and all over the world in creating families though Internet." The descriptions of the women do not say they have previously been abused, although there are a number of women whose average age is higher than most marriage agency Web sites.

There are also marriage agencies offering introduction services and pornography of women with disabilities. One site from Russia markets women with missing limbs. The services are marketed to men with fetishes for missing limbs, amputated limbs or congenital malformations. According to an amputee pornographer, "The shorter the stump is, the sexier an amputee." The photographs on the marriage agency site range from modest to sexualized. The descriptions of the women often include pledges of loyalty to a man who will take care of them. On the same agency site are photographs of orphans with disabilities. Viewers are urged to send gifts or adopt them.

Women and orphans with disabilities are extremely vulnerable. The loss of social supports following the collapse of the Soviet Union has severely worsened the circumstances for many. It would be wonderful to think of ways that people could support these women and children, but after viewing this site, one is left with a sick feeling for how they may be exploited and abused by men who offer to marry or adopt them.

MARRIAGE AND SEX TOUR AGENCIES BANNED IN THE PHILIPPINES

In the 1990s, the government of the Philippines banned the operation of marriage agencies and sex tour agencies. I don't know if there have been any prosecutions, but this new law did cause American operators of marriage agencies to move their agencies out of the Philippines. One man who operated a marriage agency complained on this Web site about this new law: "*The Philippines government is definitely working against the interests of their own people. These girls want and need to leave that country.*" Yet, he did not want to risk arrest under the new law so he withdrew from the Philippines and moved his operation to the United States. He continues his marriage agency business by using his own Filipina wife to contact and recruit women and girls in the Philippines.

MARKETING MULTIPLE FORMS OF SEXUAL EXPLOITATION

Many of the marriage agencies are part of larger commercial operations that offer a number of services, some of which are blatantly connected to the sex industry or involve the sexual exploitation of women. These multiple services include: the marriage agency, tours for men to meet women, escort services (prostitution), modelling agencies, production of pornography, and travel agencies. A number of the marriage agency Web sites have links to pornographic Web sites and prostitution services.

I documented the involvement of one marriage agency in the Philippines with sex tourism and prostitution:

> At the top of the first page of the Web site is a picture of a Filipina inviting the men to "*Come explore the Philippines with me!*" The advertisement describes the Philippines as an "*exotic and interesting place to visit.*" Information is given on tickets, lodging, food and water, money changing, nightlife and the tour schedule. Prostitution is briefly mentioned as being "*everywhere,*" and a price range for prostitutes is listed. Men are told, "*You can partake or not, it's up to you. Most do partake.*" Marriage is also briefly mentioned: "*As most of you know,*

*the Philippines is the happy hunting ground for men seeking a wife. There are all kinds of women of every description. It's hard to go to the Philippines and not get caught up in the idea of marriage. The whole lifestyle seems to revolve around love, marriage and kids."* On the next linked page the man is asked *"would you like to have a beautiful female companion as a private tour guide?"* or *"would you like to have introductions to 'decent' marriage minded ladies?"* If he chooses the private tour guide he is directed to the X-Rated Escorted Tours. At the top of this page a picture of the same Filipina from the introductory page appears, this time with her breasts exposed. The woman invites the men to *"Come explore the Philippines and Me!"* Much of the same travel information is repeated, but here the man finds out how much it costs to have an "escort" during his trip. The fee is paid to the travel agent-pimp, not the woman. The agent suggests that the sex tourist tip the woman. The viewer can also choose the marriage option and he is then directed to the linked page on *Over Seas Ladies.* There he is asked if he is tired of watching TV and having women make him jump through hoops. He is told that the women here *"respond to every gesture and kindness, no matter how small."* He is reassured that these women are not concerned about his age, appearance, or wealth. Here the man is presented with pages of pictures of women from which he can choose. The agency sells the addresses of the women to the man. For an extra fee the buyer can have a lifetime membership that entitles him to the addresses of all the women, those currently available and those in the future. (If the man is seeking a permanent relationship, why he might want or need a lifetime membership is not explained.) On the next linked page is *Escorted Wife Seeking Tours.* The man is told: *"You will meet a lot of beau4ful women there. Your penpals that you have been writing to will be happy to see you. The new women you meet will be generally 'good' girls, but there are plenty of bar girls there too and you will surely encounter some."*

Marriage agencies in Russia and Ukraine also have this type of combination of services for sexual exploitation. In addition to selling addresses of women for possible marriage, they offer to facilitate the travel of men to meet women. These agencies offer escort services (prostitution) along with the "romance" tours. Several agencies advertise that men can come and photograph women in "private nude photo sessions of Russian models" from their modeling agency. Another agency offers to take "nude" and "skin flick" photographs and videos of the women they are interested in meeting.

Several of the Russian agencies include nude photos of the women on their Web site. Some of the agency sites seem to be fully integrated into the sex industry. One example is a site that offers Russian brides, escort services, and Russian pornography. There are links on many of the agency Web sites that connect to typical sex industry (prostitution and pornography) sites.

Some of the marriage agencies and introduction services appear to operate as little more than prostitution tour agencies. The men often expect to have sex with the women. One man admitted to a reporter: "We're not here to get married." They use the marriage agency "romance tours" as sex or prostitution tourism.

## MARRIAGE AGENCIES AND SEX TRAFFICKING

It is easy to document how marriage agencies are involved in many forms of sexual exploitation and put vulnerable women and children at risk. It is harder to prove involvement of these agencies in sex trafficking as the crime is defined by law, which requires proof of force, fraud, or coercion.

Workers in the St. Petersburg Psychological Crisis Center for Women in Russia report that they have heard of women recruited by marriage agencies being trafficked into the sex industry. In Russia and other countries of the former Soviet Union, there have been so few trafficking cases prosecuted that getting detailed information on how the women were recruited is difficult. Although, information from non-governmental organizations working in these countries indicates that marriage agencies are involved in sex trafficking as well as other forms of sexual exploitation.

Some of the marriage agencies operate tour agencies that facilitate the travel and potential trafficking of women. In Chelyabinsk, Russia, an NGO representative said that the traffickers operate in travel agencies, with each agency specializing in one particular country where women are sent. In St. Petersburg, an NGO representative said that marriage agencies are well-organized business and "well protected" by the political-business-criminal networks. As in Chelyabinsk, the same people who own marriage agencies also own foreign travel and employment agencies, some of which are known to be traffickers.

One multiple service Russian agency offers to send women to meet men in other countries. If men don't want to travel to Russia, or don't want the problem of getting a visa, the agency will arrange to send a woman to another country to meet the man. It is easy to see how this could be a front for trafficking and even a way to deceive the woman into thinking she is going abroad to meet a particular man.

There are a number of aspects of these types of agencies that indicate that they are likely to be involved. 1) They have recruited a number of women who have indicated a desire to travel abroad or emigrate; 2) The women are single and able to move, although some of them may have children; 3) The women may have tried corresponding with men, meeting Western men on tours sponsored by the agencies, and now be more willing to go abroad if they agency makes them an offer; and 4) the agencies have extensive personal information about the women and their families that is often used to coerce women into prostitution once they are abroad.

One can see how an agency offering a combination of services could be involved in trafficking, especially those that essentially have a data base of information on women who are single and expressed an interest in going abroad. It is difficult to know how many of these agencies are providing the services they claim of selling addresses, and how many are involved in activities that meet the criminal definition of trafficking in women.

QUANTITATIVE RESEARCH ON MARRIAGE AGENCIES IN THE FORMER SOVIET UNION

A few years ago, I conducted a quantitative study on the recruitment of women by marriage agencies in the countries of the former Soviet Union. There is no known previous research that quantifies and maps the numbers of women recruited by "marriage agencies." The goals of this research were to determine: 1) How many Internet-based "marriage agencies" are operating in these countries? 2) How many women have been recruited by these agencies? 3) If there are particular countries, regions, and oblasts [1] from which women are being recruited? 4) Are these the same countries, regions, and oblasts from which women are known to be trafficked into sex industries? The search found almost 500 marriage agency sites with women from former Soviet republics. Two hundred and nineteen (219) of these Web sites were indexed into a database. The 219 marriage agencies had a total of 119,649 women on their sites.

Although there are large differences in the size and populations of these 15 countries, there are still noticeable differences in the recruitment of women by marriage agencies in these countries. (See Table 1 and Map 1) The countries with the largest numbers of women were the Russian Federation with over 62,000 women, followed by Ukraine with almost 32,000, and Belarus with almost 13,000. Countries with a few thousand recruited women were: Kazakhstan (3,037), Kyrgyzstan (4,190), Latvia (1,760), and Uzbekistan (1,139). The other countries had less than 1,000 recruited women: Azerbaijan (204), Estonia (551), Lithuania (626), Moldova (884), and a few countries had less than a couple of dozen women, Armenia (23), Georgia (7), Tajikistan (8), and Turkmenistan (25).

In the Russian Federation, there were large differences in the number of women recruited from each oblast. (See Table 2 and Map 2) The oblasts of Russia with the highest number of recruited women are in the western half of Russia, mostly in Europe (St. Petersburg, 15,694; Volgograd, 4,897; Moscow, 3,642, and Yekateringburg, 2,003, which straddles the European-Asian continental divide). Only ten oblasts had more than 1,000 women. St. Petersburg, with by far the highest number—almost 16,000—represented over three times the number of women recruited compared to the next closest oblasts—Volgograd in southwestern Russia with almost 4,900 and Moscow, the capital, with over 3,600. Some of the oblasts of southwestern Siberia (Omsk, 731 and Noosibirsk, 655) are the home of a moderate number of recruited women. Fewer than 100 women were recruited from 41 of the oblasts. Fewer than ten women were recruited from eleven of the oblasts (Dagestan, 8; Khakassia, 7; Alania, 4; Karachay-Cherkessia, 4; Birobijan, 3; Chita 3; Chukot, 2; Kalmykia 2; Yamalo-Nenets 2; Komi-Permyak, 1; and Tuva, 1).

There are considerable differences in population among the oblasts in Russia. The size of the difference in the number of women recruited—for example Moscow city oblast compared to oblasts in central Siberia—may partially be a reflection of the population size and density, but the numbers of recruited women are not always in direct proportion to total population.

---

[1] An oblast is an administrative division in countries of the former Soviet Union, roughly equivalent to a province or state. Ukraine is comprised of 24 oblasts and one autonomous republic. Belarus is made-up of six "voblasts," and the Russian Federation is made up of 49 oblasts, 21 republics, 10 autonomous okrugs, six krays, two federal cities, and one autonomous oblast. For simplicity, this paper will refer to administrative divisions as "oblasts" in the generic sense.

There were sizeable differences in the number of women recruited by oblast in Ukraine also. (See Table 3 and Map 3.) In Ukraine, there are a few distinct patterns for the recruitment of women by marriage agencies. The Crimea, the southern most oblast in the Black Sea, has the largest number of women recruited (5,515). Oblasts with large cities, such as the capital Kyiv (3401), Odessa (3,225), and Dnipropetrovsk (2,742) also have large numbers of women in the marriage agencies. Generally, the oblasts with the lowest numbers of recruited women are in the western Ukraine. Seven of the nine oblasts with less than 50 recruited women were in western Ukraine (Zakarpats'ka, 46; L'viv, 41; Khmelnysts'ka, 28; Volyns'ka, 24; Ternopil, 12; Ivano-Frankivsk, 10; and Rivnens'ka, 2). There is a trend that the farther east, towards Russia, you move, the more women are recruited by marriage agencies. Also, the southern oblasts on the Black Sea have fairly high numbers of women recruited from them.

In Ukraine, generally speaking, there are cultural differences between western and eastern Ukraine. Western Ukraine is more traditional and Ukrainian nationalist, while eastern Ukraine is more identified with Russian culture. How this might influence the operation and recruitment of women by marriage agencies resulting in increased recruitment of women from more Russian-identified regions is a question for further research.

Southern Ukraine has many popular resort areas. Interviews with 160 young women from Southern oblasts of Ukraine, where there was high recruitment by marriage agencies, found that two-thirds of them wanted to go abroad. Forty percent of them said they knew there was a risk of being forced into prostitution, but they were sure that it would not happen to them. In Yalta, a resort city, 97 percent of those surveyed said they wanted to go abroad. A few—six percent—said they were so eager to go abroad that they would agree to be in prostitution, even to being "sex slaves," in order to have a rich life (Hughes & Denisova 2002).

The mapping of the numbers and location of women recruited by marriage agencies reveals some distinct patterns. Clearly, there is not uniform recruitment of women across the 15 countries or within the countries. Some of the variation may be explained by population size in each of the areas, but the operation of recruiters for marriage agencies also must play a role. Likely factors contributing to the presence of recruiters are urban areas, especially tourist areas, where people have more interaction and connections to Western Europe and the U.S.—the markets for the women. This is an area that warrants further investigation.

This study was not able to link specific trafficking cases to marriage agencies for two reasons: firstly, discovering all the details of trafficking cases is difficult, and secondly, official record keeping on cases of trafficking is poor or non-existent. For example, trafficking of women was not a crime in the Russian Federation when this research was done; consequently, there are no official cases. In Ukraine, there has been a law against trafficking since 1998, but relatively few traffickers have been convicted. However, NGOs in countries of origin and destination report knowing that women are trafficked through marriage agencies.

## CONCLUSION

In countries where recruitment of women by marriage agencies is popular, the general public does not understand the risk of signing up with these agencies. A NGO worker in St. Petersburg said that her mother was urging her to sign up. She said her mother said, "Why waste your time with that work. Why not correspond with a Western man and find a better life?" She said she knew of cases in which women are afraid to go to the agencies alone, so mothers accompany their daughters to sign them up.

There is an abundance of evidence that marriage agencies are involved in activities that result in the sexual exploitation of women and children. It is harder to make links between specific marriage agencies and sex trafficking as defmed by law. There are many anecdotal reports from NGOs about the involvement of marriage agencies in the sex trafficking of women, but more investigations and collection of evidence into official cases are needed to firmly document their involvement.

TABLE 1—WOMEN RECRUITED BY MARRIAGE AGENCIES FROM COUNTRIES OF THE FORMER SOVIET UNION

| | |
|---|---|
| Armenia | 23 |
| Azerbaijan | 204 |
| Belarus | 12,683 |
| Estonia | 551 |
| Georgia | 7 |
| Kazakhstan | 3037 |
| Kyrgyzstan | 4190 |
| Latvia | 1760 |
| Lithuania | 626 |
| Moldova | 884 |
| Russian Federation | 62,605 |
| Tajikistan | 8 |
| Turkmenistan | 25 |
| Ukraine | 31,837 |
| Uzbekistan | 1,139 |
| Unknown | 70 |
| Total | 119,649 |

TABLE 2—WOMEN RECRUITED BY MARRIAGE AGENCIES IN THE RUSSIAN FEDERATION BY OBLAST

| | | | |
|---|---|---|---|
| Adygea | 18 | Moscow | 3642 |
| Alania | 4 | Murmansk | 43 |
| Altai | 73 | Nizhniy Novgorod | 178 |
| Amur | 25 | Novgorod | 502 |
| Arkhangelsk | 253 | Novosibirsk | 655 |
| Astrakhan’ | 429 | Omsk | 731 |
| Bashkortostan | 440 | Orel Oblast | 72 |
| Belgorod | 86 | Orenburg | 96 |
| Birobijan | 3 | Penza | 311 |
| Bryansk | 69 | Mordovia | 14 |
| Buryatia | 15 | Perm | 221 |
| Chelyabinsk | 474 | Primorskiy | 645 |
| Chita | 3 | Pskov | 55 |
| Chukot | 2 | Rostov | 1044 |
| Chuvashia | 154 | Ryazan’ | 282 |
| Dagestan | 8 | Sakhalin | 178 |
| lrkutsk | 133 | Samara | 1510 |
| Ivanovo | 32 | Saratov | 2344 |
| Kabardino-Balkaria | 22 | Smolensk | 23 |
| Kaliningrad | 295 | St. Petersburg | 15694 |
| Kalmykia | 2 | Stavropol | 365 |
| Kaluga | 72 | Tambov | 111 |
| Kamchatka | 27 | Tatarstan | 2165 |
| Karachay-Cherkessia | 4 | Taymyr | 31 |
| Karelia | 49 | Tomsk | 235 |
| Kemerovo | 173 | Tula | 43 |
| Khabarovsk | 313 | Tuva | 1 |
| Khakassia | 7 | Tver | 1373 |
| Khanty-Mansi | 41 | Tyumen | 159 |
| Kirov | 26 | Udmurtia | 317 |
| Komi | 203 | Ul’yanovsk | 280 |
| Komi-Permyak | 1 | Vladimir | 58 |
| Kostroma | 10 | Volgograd | 4897 |
| Krasnodar | 834 | Vologda | 60 |

| | | | |
|---|---|---|---|
| Krasnoyarsk | 175 | Voronezh | 121 |
| Kurgan | 82 | Yakutia | 21 |
| Kursk | 27 | Yamalo-Nenets | 2 |
| Lipetsk | 82 | Yaroslavl | 64 |
| Magadan | 22 | Yekateringburg | 2003 |
| Mari-El | 1869 | Not Known | 14967 |
| | | Total | 62605 |

TABLE 3—WOMEN RECRUITED BY MARRIAGE AGENCIES IN UKRAINE, BY OBLAST

| | | | |
|---|---|---|---|
| Cherkas'ka | 149 | Mykolayiv | 533 |
| Chernivhivs'ka | 35 | Odessa | 3225 |
| Chernivitsi | 268 | Poltava | 368 |
| Dnipropetrovsk | 2742 | Respublika Krym | 551 |
| Donetsk | 1055 | Rivnens'ka | 2 |
| Ivano-Frankivsk | 10 | Sums'ka | 1994 |
| Kharkivs'ka | 1188 | Ternopil' | 12 |
| Khersons'ka | 1053 | Vinnytsya | 440 |
| Khmelnyts'ka | 28 | Volyns'ka | 24 |
| Kiev | 3401 | Zakarpats'ka | 46 |
| Kirovohrads'ka | 10 | Zaporizhzhya | 539 |
| Luhans'ka | 281 | Zhytomyr | 125 |
| L'viv | 41 | Unknown | 8753 |
| | | Total | 31837 |

Map 1

Women Recruited by Marriage Agencies in Countries of the Former Soviet Union

**Map 2**
**Women Recruited by Marriage Agencies in the Russian Federation, by Oblast**

Map 3

**Women Recruited by Marriage Agencies in Ukraine, by Oblast**

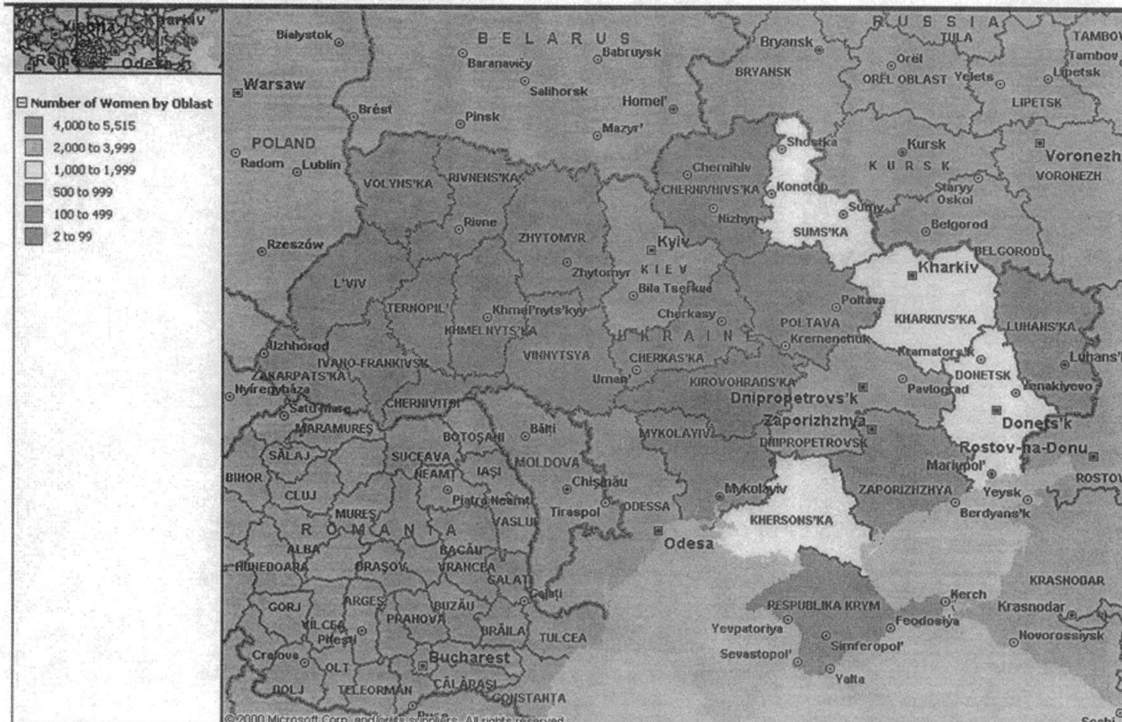

REFERENCES

Hughes, Donna M. "Supplying Women for the Sex Industry: Trafficking from the Russian Federation," in *Sexualities in Post-Communism,* Aleksandar Stulhofer (Editor) Haworth Press (Forthcoming) http://www.uri.edu/artsci/wms/hughes/supplying__women.pdf

Hughes, Donna M. 2004. "The Role of 'Marriage Agencies' in the Sexual Exploitation of Women from the Former Soviet Union," *International Review of Victimology,* Vol. 11, pp. 49-71.

Hughes, Donna M. 2003. *The Impact of the Use of New Communications and Information Technologies on the Trafficking of Women: A Study of the Users,* The Group of Specialists on the Impact of the Use of New Information Technologies on Trafficking in Human Beings for the Purpose of Sexual Exploitation, Committee for Equality between Women and Men, Council of Europe. http://www.uri.edu/artsci/wms/hughes/eg-n-st__flnal__report.doc

"Marriage agencies and images," Nov 2001
http://www.uri.edu/artsci/wms/hughes/agencies__and__images.pdf

Hughes, Donna M. 2002. "Use of New Information and Communication Technologies for Sexual Exploitation of Women and Children," *Hastings Women's Law Journal,* Vol. 13, No. 1, pp. 129-148.

Hughes, Donna M. July 2002. *Trafficking for Sexual Exploitation: The Case of the Russian Federation,* IOM Migration Research Series, International Organization for Migration, No. 7, 68 pages. http://www.uri.edu/artsci/wms/hughes/russia.pdf

Hughes, Donna M. and Tatyana A. Denisova, "The Transnational Political Criminal Nexus of Trafficking of Women in Ukraine," *Trends in Organized Crime* Vol. 6, No. 3-4: Spr.-Sum. 2001 (Printing date March 2003) http://www.uri.edu/artsci/wms/hughes/tpcnexus.pdf

Hughes, Donna M. 1999. *Pimps and Predators on the Internet—Globalizing the Sexual Exploitation of Women and Children.* Kingston, Rhode Island: The Coalition Against Trafficking in Women, 80 pages. ISBN 0-9670857-1-3 http://www.uri.edu/artsci/wms/hughes/pprep.pdf

Senator BROWNBACK. Thank you very much.

Do you know what is an average price for brokering? Have you been able to track that?

Dr. HUGHES. Well, they usually charge anywhere from $10 to $15 per address or sometimes they will say, but then you can have 15 addresses for $100. Sometimes they have deals of lifetime memberships, although what you would need a lifetime membership for, if you are supposedly seeking a wife, I am not sure. Of course, then they offer tours for the men to go on to meet the women, either the ones they have been corresponding with or women they have never met before, and those can be the price of an airline ticket plus the hotels plus whatever profit they are able to put on top of it. So I think it is important to understand that a lot of these agencies are making money any way they can, whether it is selling addresses, providing women for prostitution, maybe trafficking the women abroad, even making money doing things like delivering flowers for the man and making a profit on top of that.

Senator BROWNBACK. And what do the women get out of this or charge?

Dr. HUGHES. They usually are not charged anything.

Senator BROWNBACK. So they are offering themselves and putting themselves in harm's way.

Dr. HUGHES. Right, in the hope of meeting Mr. Right.

Senator BROWNBACK. Ms. Jackson.

**STATEMENT OF SUZANNE H. JACKSON, ASSOCIATE PROFESSOR OF CLINICAL LAW, GEORGE WASHINGTON UNIVERSITY LAW SCHOOL**

Ms. JACKSON. Thank you Senator Brownback, Senator Cantwell, and to the rest of the committee for the opportunity to testify today.

Before becoming a law professor, I worked as an attorney here in the District of Columbia representing immigrants and refugees seeking to escape abusive relationships. Most of my clients did not speak much English and had to overcome many obstacles before they could escape domestic violence. Two of my clients had met their husbands through mail order bride companies, and it is because of the particular hardships that they endured that I began researching this issue when I entered academia. The legal landscape facing women in this situation has changed dramatically since those days, in no small part due to the excellent work of this committee in the hearings upon and shaping of the Trafficking Victims Protection Act of 2000.

The IMOs, or international matchmaking organizations, have been linked to criminal trafficking in several ways. They can be nothing more than fronts for criminal trafficking organizations in which adults and girls are offered to the public as brides, but sold privately into prostitution or forced marriage—including marriages to men who prostitute them—or held in domestic slavery. Global Survival Network found that most mail order bride agencies in Russia have expanded their activities to include trafficking for prostitution. European embassies have reported that a number of matchmaking agencies conceal organized prostitution rings victimizing newly arrived Filipina women. Asian groups have used fiancée visas and marriage with a so-called jockey, which is an escort bringing women across the U.S. border, to bring women into the United States for purposes of prostitution. And jockeys have even included U.S. military personnel stationed abroad.

IMOs' practices exacerbate problems with false expectations, requiring women to complete long questionnaires with very intrusive and detailed personal questions, encouraging disclosure by implying or stating that false answers could lead to cancellation of any ensuing immigration benefits. Women are also subjected to medical and background checks and may assume that participating men are evaluated with the same level of scrutiny. Women from other countries often assume that all governmental agencies in the United States, a country with extraordinary resources and technology, have access to information held by other agencies, that facts asserted in applications for immigration benefits would be checked, and that a man who had been convicted of serious violent crimes would not be permitted to bring a spouse or fiancée into the U.S. from abroad. The industry does nothing, however, to screen male customers, no detailed questionnaire, no check for a criminal record or abuse, no formal inquiry as to whether men are already married. Until recently, the U.S. Government did not conduct these inquiries either.

An IMO can also be a useful tool of and a collaborator with individual men who seek to exploit women whom they import to the United States. U.S. citizens can use isolation, domination, and threats of deportation to get an immigrant woman to perform domestic and sexual services on demand. One commentator in an Internet discussion of the pros and cons of paying for a mail order bride pointed out that it can be much less expensive to purchase a wife than to pay for prostitution services which do not typically include free housekeeping and cooking.

Men have also used imprisonment and vicious violence to sexually exploit and prostitute young women. One Honduran woman was kept a prisoner, together with the U.S. citizen's wife, in a man's home by bars on the windows. Another was kept in the house on an ankle chain. One 17-year-old from the Philippines was abused, sexually exploited, and then pimped into prostitution.

The CIA found that the mail order bride brokers are not traffickers per se, but when there is deception or fraudulent nondisclosure of known facts concerning the nature of the relationship being entered into or the criminal or abusive background of the client—that is the male client—the broker should be liable as traffickers. Individuals using IMOs to find women whom they prostitute to others or who they use as their own personal prostitutes or domestic servants should be criminally liable as traffickers on the same theory. Knowing deception or fraud used intentionally to persuade a woman or girl to travel to the United States and perhaps even to marry, in order to mistreat and exploit her for personal profit or gain, is no less criminal trafficking in persons when accomplished by an individual instead of an organization. Although the Department of Justice is enforcing criminal laws against international travel for purposes of having sex with a child, not one sex trafficking case has been brought against an individual who has used a mail order bride agency to obtain and sexually exploit a vulnerable immigrant woman. It could be that the case that you mentioned at the beginning would have been an exception to that had the man not committed suicide.

Commercial sex is defined in the Trafficking Victims Protection act as any sex act on account of which anything of value is given or received by any person. When an IMO sells a young woman for sexual purposes, as in a Web page openly offering sex with 15- to 17-year-old Thai girls boasting that a girl could be delivered anywhere in the world, charging extra to deliver a virgin, and also offering that if the customer paid $4,000 more, then she is like your slave forever, this is clearly commercial sex trafficking. But when a citizen threatens to——

Senator BROWNBACK. Excuse me. Let me just stop you there. What are the prices that they are putting there in that section you were talking about?

Ms. JACKSON. It is $4,000 for delivery of a young, underage girl for sexual purposes, and for an additional $4,000, she is your slave forever.

Senator BROWNBACK. So $8,000 for a slave, female sex slave basically.

Ms. JACKSON. That is right. And that is less than it takes for an individual to go and get a mail order bride—that is more actually. That is about double what it takes for an individual to go and get a mail order bride from any other country to bring her into the

United States, even including the fees to the trafficking organizations.

When a citizen threatens to revoke an application for a green card unless an immigrant submits to sex, the valuable consideration of legal residency in the U.S. fulfills both the commercial sex requirement and the coercion requirement of the criminal sex trafficking statute.

I have one last point to make.

Senator BROWNBACK. Please go ahead.

Ms. JACKSON. During the 1970s and 1980s, an average of 5,300 fiancée petitions were filed each year, about 1,100 of which did not result in an adjustment of status to permanent residents. So these are people who got in as fiancées who were not made wives. During the 1990s, the number of fiancée petitions rose to 6,400 a year, while the number of adjustments remained the same. So the missing or rejected fiancées between the 1970s and the 1980s, and the 1990s, doubled. There was no increase in the number of people who were adjusted to permanent residents. The INS in a report acknowledged that foreign traffickers are attracted to the United States because of the ability to get fiancée visas, but in that report they never connected the doubling of the number of fiancée visas and the failure to turn those into spouses as evidence itself of sex trafficking in women.

The proposals that have been made to improve the situation regarding matchmaking organizations are excellent and should place minimal burdens on individuals and the companies. But if regulations are not in place to ensure that Congress' enactments have the force of law, the study that is proposed by Senator Cantwell and other reforms contemplated will be meaningless. In the June 23, 2004 Federal Register, the notice of proposed rulemaking for a law passed in 1996 to require IMOs to give mail order brides information about their rights in the United States will not be issued until sometime in December of this year. That is 8 years since the final comment period ended on that regulation. Even though there have been regulations passed to control the IMO industry, they are not being enforced. They have not been implemented by the executive, and without that, the laws themselves might as well not have been written.

I thank you for the committee's efforts to combat trafficking and abuses of the international matchmaking industry and for your consideration of my testimony.

[The prepared statement of Ms. Jackson follows:]

PREPARED STATEMENT OF SUZANNE H. JACKSON

Thank you to Senator Brownback and to the rest of the Committee for the opportunity to testify today. My name is Suzanne Jackson, and I am an Associate Professor of Clinical Law at George Washington Law School. Before becoming a law professor, I worked as an attorney here in the District of Columbia, representing immigrants and refugees seeking to escape abusive relationships. Most of my clients did not speak much English, and had to overcome many obstacles before they could be free of the threat of domestic violence. Two of my clients had met their husbands through "mail-order bride" companies, and it is because of the particular hardships they endured within the legal system that I began to research the relationship between the "mail-order bride" industry and trafficking in women. The legal landscape has, on the whole, improved significantly since those days, thanks in great part to the work of this Committee in conducting hearings on and shaping the Trafficking Victims Protection Act of 2000.

I will refer to the companies as international matchmaking organizations or IMOs rather than "mail-order bride" agencies, even though the term IMO inaccurately conveys gender neutrality and a "match" or some level of equality between the parties. Nothing could be further from the truth: IMOs exist for the benefit of their paying customers: men [1] from wealthy nations, including the United States, Japan and Germany, who want access to women who, most often, have neither economic nor social power. Marketing strategies used by IMOs advertise women as generic to their ethnicity—all Russian women are X, all Asian women are Y, all Latinas are Z—and emphasize that the women they offer (women who are in fact hoping to leave their home countries) will all be "home-oriented" and "traditional" wives. Some companies guarantee women's availability, others guarantee marriage within a year of subscribing to their service, one even allows a man to remove a woman from the Web site to prevent competition during a courtship: "Select One, She's Yours," promises this company.[2]

IMOs have been linked to criminal trafficking in several ways. They can be nothing more than fronts for criminal trafficking organizations, in which adults and girls are offered to the public as brides but sold privately into prostitution, forced into marriage (including marriages to men who then prostitute them),[3] or held in domestic slavery. Police in the United Kingdom found organized criminal gangs from Russia, the former Soviet Union and the Balkans using the Internet to advertise women for sale to brothels in Western Europe and also to men as "Internet brides."[4] A study by Global Survival Network (GSN) found that most mail-order bride agencies in Russia have expanded their activities to include trafficking for prostitution. European embassies have reported that a number of matchmaking agencies conceal organized prostitution rings victimizing newly-arrived Filipina women. Asian groups have used fiancée visas and marriage with a so-called "jockey" (an escort bringing women across the U.S. border) to bring women into the U.S. for purposes of prostitution;[5] jockeys have even included U.S. military personnel posted abroad.

IMOs are almost completely unregulated, advertise minors for marriage, and fail to screen their male clients for criminal histories. with false expectations: they require women to complete long questionnaires asking intrusive personal questions, encouraging disclosure by implying or stating that false answers could lead to cancellation of any ensuing immigration benefits. Women are also subjected to medical and background checks, and may assume that participating men are evaluated with the same level of scrutiny. Women from other countries often assume that all governmental agencies in the United States—a country with extraordinary resources and technology—have access to information held by other agencies, that facts asserted in applications for immigration benefits would be checked, and that a man who had been convicted of serious violent crimes would not be permitted to bring a spouse or fiancée into the U.S. from abroad. The industry does nothing, however, to screen male customers: no detailed questionnaire, no check for a criminal record for spousal or child abuse, no formal inquiry as to whether men are already married. Until recently, the U.S. government also did not conduct these inquiries.

An IMO can also be a useful tool of, and sometimes a knowing collaborator with, an individual man who wishes to obtain control over a woman in order to exploit her. A U.S. citizen can use isolation, domination, and threats of deportation to get an immigrant woman to perform domestic and sexual services on demand. One commentator in an Internet discussion of the pros and cons of paying for a "mail-order" bride, pointed out that it can be much less expensive to purchase a wife than to pay for prostitution services, which don't also include free housekeeping and cooking. Men have also used imprisonment and vicious violence to sexually exploit and prostitute young women. One Honduran woman was kept a prisoner—together with the U.S. citizen's wife—in a man's home by bars on the windows; another was kept in the house on an ankle chain; one 17-year old from the Phillipines was abused, sexually exploited, and then pimped into prostitution.[6]

Because of these practices, the CIA found that "[m]ail order bride brokers . . . are not traffickers per se; but, where there is deception or fraudulent non-disclosure of known facts concerning the nature of the relationship being entered into or the criminal or abusive background of the client, the brokers should be liable as traffickers."[7] Individuals using IMOs to find women whom they prostitute to others or use as their own "personal prostitutes"[8] or domestic servants should be criminally liable as traffickers on the same theory. Knowing deception—fraud—used intentionally to cause a woman or girl to travel to the U.S. and perhaps even to marry, in order to mistreat and exploit her for personal profit or gain, is no less criminal trafficking in persons when accomplished by an individual instead of an organization. Although the Department of Justice is enforcing the criminal laws against international travel for purposes of having sex with a child, not one sex trafficking case has been brought against an individual who has used a mail-order bride organization to obtain and sexually exploit a vulnerable immigrant woman.[9]

Abusive IMO-arranged marriages should be evaluated for evidence of criminal trafficking. Consider the following examples:

- A U.S. citizen puts new locks on the outside of his doors, and installs a security system with keyed window locks. He searches the Internet for the youngest possible girls available on mail-order bride Web sites. He pays a company's $4,500 fee, travels abroad, proposes marriage to a young woman, and brings his prospective wife to the U.S. with a fiancée visa. When they arrive at his home, he takes her down to the basement and terrorizes her, keeping her locked there for weeks. When he believes that she is too afraid to try to escape, he allows her out of the basement but not out of the house, forcing her to do housework and have sex with him on demand.
- A U.S. citizen lives in a remote, rural area, and accomplishes the above with repeated physical and sexual abuse, but without need for locks, as the nearest house is thirty miles away.
- Add to the facts in both scenarios above that the citizen forces a woman to have sex with other men who pay him for the privilege.
- Add to the facts in any scenario that instead of using a fiancée visa to "secure a woman's entry into the U.S., the man marries her abroad and brings her to the U.S. as his wife.

These scenarios, distilled from actual cases,[10] all fulfill the elements of the federal crime of forced labor: domestic labor or sexual services intentionally obtained by the use of physical restraint and threats of serious harm. They should also satisfy the elements of criminal sex trafficking, if the required element of "commercial sex act" is interpreted on the basis of the statutory language rather than a myopic intepretation focusing exclusively on brothel-based prostitution or monetary transactions.

Commercial sex is defined in the Trafficking Victims Protection Act as "any sex act, on account of which anything of value is given to or received by any person." When an with fifteen- to seventeen-year old Thai girls, boasting that a girl could be delivered "anywhere in the world," charging extra to deliver a virgin, and also offered girls for sale outright—pay $4,000 more, the company promised, "and then she is like your slave forever." [11]—this is clearly commercial sex trafficking. If both parties to the sale know that the person will be forced or coerced to have sex, both are sex traffickers. The formality of a marriage or a supposed engagement to marry should not blind us to the federal crimes of sex trafficking, forced labor and involuntary servitude: when a citizen threatens to revoke an application for a green card unless an immigrant submits to sex, the valuable consideration of legal residency in the United States fulfills both the "commercial sex" requirement and the coercion requirement of the criminal sex trafficking statute. The same applies in the context of sexual exploitation of domestic workers, migrant workers, sweatshop workers, or any instance where sex is coerced or forced through threats of deportation, so that a person is led to believe that on account of the sex act, the person will receive respite from threats of deportation.[12] The criminal penalties for sex trafficking should be brought to bear against individuals who use IMOs to extort sex and domestic services from individual brought into the U.S. through fiancée visas or through marriage.

IMOs also camouflage trafficking indirectly by inflating the number of visa applicants, which reduces governmental resources to evaluate individuals' requests for fiancée visas. Until recently, U.S. immigration authorities conducted no investigation of applicants for fiancée or spousal visas, not requiring any background criminal check, not asking whether the petitioner is legally able to marry, not even checking its own records to see if an applicant previously petitioned for another person. During the 1970s and 1980s, an average of 5,300 fiancée petitions were filed each year, about 1,100 of which did not result in an adjustment to permanent resident status. During the 1990s, however, the number of fiancée petitions rose to 6,400 per year while adjustments remained the same. The number of missing or rejected fiancées had apparently doubled in a decade, averaging about 2,200 a year. A report by the INS noted that traffickers were interested in sending women to the U.S. because fiancée visas were easy to obtain, but did not observe that the rise in "missing" or rejected fiancées was itself evidence of trafficking.[13] Since the tragedy of September 11th, the Bureau of Citizenship and Immigration Services has increased scrutiny of all petitioners and beneficiaries of petitions for immigration benefits, including petitions for fiancée visas and marriage-based adjustment, and although implementation of these changes is only just beginning, they have reportedly already found much of interest as a result of these investigations.

Senator Cantwell has made several excellent proposals to change the process for obtaining a fiancée visa, which if enacted and implemented would place minimal burdens on the IMOs and on the participants in the process, while likely preventing some serious abuses of the system. But even enacting such a law will accomplish nothing if Congress is not prepared to ensure that the laws are implemented by the Executive Branch. This is not the first piece of legislation recognizing and attempting to address problems in the U.S. that Congress in 1996 ordered IMOs to provide information to their "recruits" on their rights under U.S. laws. Eight years later, this law is still not implemented or enforced.[14] The comment period for the proposed regulation expired in 1997, yet the June 23, 2004 *Federal Register* announced that the Notice of Proposed Rulemaking will not be issued until sometime in December of this year. Senator Cantwell's legislation asks the Bureau of Citizenship and Immigration Services to complete a study of the industry and the extent of its compliance with the new requirements within two years of the legislation's enactment, but if the regulations are not in place to ensure that Congress' enactments have the force of law, this study and the other reforms contemplated, will be meaningless.

Thank you for the Committee's efforts to combat trafficking and abuses of the international matchmaking industry, for the invitation to appear before you today, and for your consideration of my testimony.

NOTES

[1] In three years of research I identified only two Web sites purporting to offer "mail-order husbands," one of which was defunct, and the other a satire. Although one or two sites listed at Mail Order Bride Warehouse (www.goodwife.com) had listings for both men and women, over 350 sites (in 2002) provided only listings of women for review by male customers.

[2] *The Mail Order Bride Latin Page,* at http://www.goodwife.com/latin (last visited Aug. 15, 2002).

[3] In a recent study of trafficked women in the U.S., experts interviewed forty trafficked women, finding that "[h]usbands and boyfriends acted as pimps for some of the international (20%) and U.S. (28%) women. Coalition Against Trafficking in Women, "Sex Trafficking," at 10. One of these women had been sold into marriage.

[4] Miller, *Sex Gangs Sell Prostitutes over the Internet,* The Guardian (U.K.), July 16, 2000, at 13.

[5] Amy O'Neill Richard, Center for the Study of Intelligence, International Trafficking in Women to the United States: A Contemporary Manifestation of Slavery and Organized Crime (Nov. 1999), at 8.

[6] See Suzanne H. Jackson, *To Honor and Obey: Trafficking in "Mail-order Brides,"* 70 George Wash. L. Rev. 475, at notes 560-563 (June 2002).

[7] Amy O'Neill Richard, "International Trafficking in Women to the United States: A Contemporary Manifestation of Slavery and Organized Crime," Center for the Study of Intelligence, November, 1999, citing Ali Miller and Alison Stewart, "Report from the Roundtable on the Meaning of Trafficking in Persons: A Human Rights Perspective," Women's Rights Law Reporter, Rugtgers Law School Fall/Winter 1998. The INS agreed. "International Matchmaking Organizations: A Report to Congress," at 17-18 (March, 1999).

[8] The phrase "personal prostitute" was used by a reporter to describe a fifteen-year old Costa Rican boy brought into Florida for sex by a much older man, Marvin Hersh. The case against Mr. Hersh is described in my article cited above, text accompanying notes 617-632.

[9] Conversation with Professor Mohammed Mattar, Protection Project, Johns Hopkins University, July 12, 2004. Professor Mattar has reviewed the cases brought by the Department of Justice under the Trafficking Victims Protection Act.

[10] Jackson, *To Honor and Obey,* supra note 6, at notes 560-563.

[11] Stuart Miller, *Sex Gangs Sell Prostitutes over the Internet,* The Guardian (U.K.), July 16, 2000, at 13.

[12] The requirement that some action occur in interstate commerce will limit this provision to instances when an intent to extort sex existed before the person is brought to the U.S., or whe course of conduct extends across state lines. This stops the definition of sex trafficking from encompassing all IMO-arranged relationships, regardless of the parties' intent.

[13] "International Matchmaking Organizations: A Report to Congress," at 10 (March, 1999). Some level of oversight has been exercised, however, as one IMO agent complained: "The [IMO] service itself is not restricted by the American government, although they are real picky about getting your bride into the states—they

won't give a visa to a bride under age sixteen." Donna M. Hughes, "Pimps and Predators on the Internet: Globalizing the Sexual Exploitation of Women and Children," Coalition Against Trafficking in Women, March 1999, citing "Be a Mail Order Husband (For Men Only)," World Class Service, 1996, available at http://www.filipina.com/FAQ.html.

[14] *See, e.g.,* "Kohl Urges I.N.S. to Crack Down on 'Mail-Order Bride' Industry," Press Release, Senator Herb Kohl, February 9, 2001. "The INS has ignored the law. It has been dragging its feet. By not doing its job, it has allowed the mail-order bride industry to flourish unchecked and rife with abuse. Meanwhile, more women walk blindly into these marriages with little or no information about their rights. The rules are in place. All the INS has to do is enforce them to prevent another senseless tragedy." Id.

Senator BROWNBACK. Thank you.

Is this is a largely or completely unregulated industry, the international matchmaking organizations?

Ms. JACKSON. The only regulation that exists has not yet been implemented by the United States.

Senator BROWNBACK. That one that you were citing to is the only one that you know of. Is that true of most countries or are we behind in the industrialized countries, or are we ahead and nobody is really looking at this?

Ms. JACKSON. It is true of most countries, but we are behind most industrialized countries, particularly the EU, and I would defer to Professors Hughes and perhaps Clark in terms of the most up-to-date information about other countries' efforts in thess areas, but I think that these industries are more severely regulated and recognized as different forms of trafficking in other countries.

Senator BROWNBACK. That is going to lead to my next question, which maybe you could combine with this one. What have other governments done on this topic that we should learn from and try to address?

Ms. CLARK. None that I have been able to find. We do note that the Council of Europe has recently pointed to the lack of regulation of the industry and, in its April 2004 report on domestic slavery, is calling for further recommendations. But we have yet to see it. I was in Norway in April and heard about a story of a Norwegian man in the north who was just about to get his 13th mail order bride from Russia, and there was no law that could prevent this from happening. He would bring the women in. He would stay married to them until almost the end of their trial period, until just weeks before they would automatically obtain residency, divorce them—occasionally they already had children—and then file for his next mail order bride. There was nothing in the existing regulation to prevent him from going for bride number 20.

Dr. HUGHES. As I said in my testimony, the Philippines does have a law against the operation of mail order bride agencies. There was sort of a coinciding of events. During the 1980s, almost all mail order brides came from Southeast Asia, particularly from the Philippines and Thailand. The Philippines passed a law against the operation of these agencies which caused the Americans that were onsite in the Philippines to come back to the United States with their computers and then have to send recruiters in. But also, there was then the collapse of the Soviet Union that opened up the borders, and a lot of the marriage brokers then moved to eastern Europe. And now you will find that the vast majority of women offered in these sites are from the countries of the former Soviet Union.

One of the things I will mention in the research that I did on mail order bride agencies in the former Soviet Union, we indexed 219 agencies and found 120,000 women in those 219 agencies.

Senator BROWNBACK. How many women?

Dr. HUGHES. It is 119,649, just under 120,000 women on over 200 marriage sites.

Senator BROWNBACK. Dr. Hughes, go into more detail about the nature of these tours. I do not know what they call them, engagement tours or whatever.

Dr. HUGHES. They call them romance tours, but I think they are really often little more than sex tours because I have read a number of accounts in which the men talk about how they go on one of these tours a couple times a year. So it really is a sex tour. The women on the other end may think these men are coming to meet them and possibly marry them, but the men, in effect, are really just going there to have sex and have a good time for a week or so, and then they come back.

Senator BROWNBACK. Where are these tours generally to? What is the price? How are they advertised?

Dr. HUGHES. I have seen a number of them to Kiev, St. Petersburg, Moscow. They are the popular destinations in the former Soviet Union. I have also seen them to Manila and to Costa Rica. So almost anywhere there is a significant operation of either sex tours and the combination of these mail order bride agencies, they will run what are called these romance tours.

I think what is really interesting is you look at how often these agencies are combination agencies, everything from the marriage agencies, sex tour agents, running prostitution rings, travel agencies, tour agencies, and they produce pornography, and all of that sort of comes together. I think that they then use the women any way that they can.

Senator BROWNBACK. So this is just a criminal conglomerate.

Dr. HUGHES. I think so.

Senator BROWNBACK. It is what it is, and they use marriage as some sort of legitimacy front to a multifaceted sex industry organization.

Dr. HUGHES. Yes, I think so. I think especially when you realize that by running a mail order bride agency, if you put all the ads in the newspapers, you suddenly have several hundred women from the community that have signed up. And now you know where there are 200 women from that community that have expressed an interest in going abroad. I could see how it would work that the trafficker says, OK, you can correspond with an American man or a while and a couple months go by and nothing has really happened. Then he can say, you know, I heard there is this really good job abroad working as a waitress in a restaurant. It is a really high class restaurant. I am sure you would meet a man right away if you went there, and we can help find you a husband that way. But, of course, when she reaches the destination, she is forced into prostitution.

Ms. CLARK. There are events where they have invited women to meet men on these tours, and they are simultaneously soliciting the women for jobs abroad. That has been noted particularly in Russia.

Also in Australia I believe there is a law that assisted the government to prosecute a man who brought over his seventh mail order bride. But I think that current criminal laws against immigration fraud could be used in that way because those petitions are not made in good faith.

Ms. CLARK. We agree that the mail order bride industry is becoming an increasingly large cover for forms of sex tourism, and I would agree with Dr. Hughes. In our research on brides of Central Asia, we have seen this where men would post testimonies of how they had had vacations. On their summer vacations, they would go and visit the homes of six or eight women. Frequently the families would go all out to welcome the men into their homes because this was potentially a way for the woman to leave and maybe even for her whole family. The man would return to the United States, post a notice on the Web site saying this was a lovely trip, I enjoyed meeting everybody, I did not find my soul mate, but I will be back again next year. The NGOs in Kyrgystan would then tell us that in fact these women were multiply used by the men who would come through because they felt again reduced to a commodity and that the men felt it was their right to try out what perhaps they might purchase.

So in discussions, I think that as we examine the types of prevention campaigns that we are continuing to fund in countries of origin, these types of practices need to be made more explicit, in that the idea of responding to an ad for marriage is not necessarily the dream that it might appear to be.

Senator BROWNBACK. So this is one of the next great fronts in the modern-day slavery debate and practices we are seeing?

Ms. CLARK. I would say so. I would say in general the use of the Internet needs to be studied with much greater dedication to see exactly how it is being used. The abuse of the mail order bride industry is something that we are documenting today, but with the rise of an online community, we are starting to see in an American suburb outside of the town of Peoria that a man can plug in: Peoria, the ZIP code, young girls 14 to 18, and get 900 profiles of young girls who are talking about the things that they love, their wants, their desires, their dreams.

Many of us in the room are familiar with the case of Lindsey Lavoy, a young woman who met someone through an online community chat room in Miami in August 2000 I believe, who introduced himself as a 15-year-old who, just like her, loved poetry. A few months later he revealed, one, that he loved her but, by the way, he was 35. The end of the tragic story is that she was convinced to leave with him, was taken to Greece, and was put into the pornographic film industry there.

So these online communities, in ways very similar to the mail order bride industry, are now being increasingly used as potential recruitment stations and auction blocks. This is something that is not regulated, but deserves very focused attention as part of the overall war against trafficking, Senator.

Senator BROWNBACK. Ms. Jackson, you talked about jockeys getting married many times. I believe that was in your testimony.

Ms. JACKSON. It was not that they were getting married many times, but I think the specifics of the incident that I was describing were servicemen in Korea were being paid between $30,000 and $40,000 to marry a Korean woman, bring her to the United States, remain with her for the 2 years needed to get her permanent residence here, and then divorce her. The understanding was that there would be severe sanctions to pay for the man if he laid a finger on the woman because they wanted to keep her safe for an eventual true marriage, but the money was too difficult to resist for these young men.

Senator BROWNBACK. Dr. Hughes, that is the strangest thing you were talking about, about missing body parts and people's fetishes. These are actually Internet sites?

Dr. HUGHES. A couple of years ago, the Council of Europe commissioned me to do research on how the Internet is being used to traffic women, and this was actually some of the work that I did. I got into some very dark sides of the Internet. This was one particular site that I found, which was a combination of a sort of pornography site and a marriage agency in which they were essentially recruiting women throughout Russia that had disabilities because there are men who are known to have sexual fetishes for women with disabilities. They were actually marketing these women. The women pathetically would have pledges on the site for anyone who would be willing to take care of them. They would promise to be loyal to them and so forth.

Senator BROWNBACK. That is just unbelievable. I have seen a lot of terrible things, evil things in the world, but that is just unbelievable.

I hope you have all put in your written testimony specific items of what you think we should be doing, either amending current trafficking laws or the Cantwell proposal that she has put forward. It strikes me that this is the logical place we would probably be at this point in time in the trafficking that was begun several years back. We have finally recognized it and then moved on laws against it, and then you would see probably other groups then morph into a different way or to get more sophisticated about what they were doing and still trying to address a potential market, a substantial market. So it seems to me that we have to be then moving with how the industry is moving to address it and to address it as carefully as we can and as well as we can and allowing legitimate groups to operate, but illegitimate ones to really suffer the consequences.

I hope also we can start to put on notice vulnerable female populations in other countries and people here of right and wrong and things that they should be watching out for.

I hope each of you will be willing to work with us as we try to craft through how it is we would do something along these lines.

I was glad to see Director Miller stayed through the panel's presentation because he is on the front line in our efforts here within the executive branch and we here in the legislative branch.

Anything else, ladies, that you would like to let us know about that we should know about?

If not, thank you very much for the testimony. We will look forward to working with you on addressing this problem.

The hearing is adjourned.

[Whereupon, at 4:08 p.m., the subcommittee adjourned, to reconvene subject to the call of the Chair.]

○